IN THE
LION'S DEN

ISRAEL AND THE WORLD

DANNY DANON

WICKED SON

A WICKED SON BOOK
An Imprint of Post Hill Press
ISBN: 978-1-63758-000-4
ISBN (eBook): 978-1-63758-001-1

In the Lion's Den:
Israel and the World
© 2022 by Danny Danon
All Rights Reserved

Cover Design by Tiffani Shea

Post Hill Press
New York • Nashville
posthillpress.com

Published in the United States of America
2 3 4 5 6 7 8 9 10

To my beloved wife, Talie, and our beautiful children,
Aviad, Hila, and Shira, who are inspiring
partners in all of my endeavors.

CONTENTS

A Faithful Friend in a Sea of Enemies

The United Nations is not for the faint of heart. It's a place where dictators, murderers, and thieves denounce America and our allies, then turn around and demand that we pay their bills. It was the privilege of a lifetime to shake things up as America's ambassador. And it was a pleasure to do so alongside my friend and fellow ambassador, Danny Danon.

I met Danny right away at the UN—and that was a big deal. Normal protocol is for American ambassadors to have their first meetings with members of the Security Council, including Russia and Communist China. But I wanted to prioritize Israel—our friend—ahead of our enemies. The reason was simple: One month earlier, America had abandoned Israel at the UN. The previous administration had abstained in a vote condemning Israeli settlements, allowing the biased and bigoted measure to pass. I wanted Israel to know that America once again had its back.

It was immediately clear that he and I would have a great working relationship. We share the same values, including defending our respective countries. We share the same skepticism of the UN, recognizing the deck is stacked against the principles we hold dear. Finally, we share the same direct approach. Danny and I knew we had to fight, and fight hard, to accomplish anything positive in such a negative place.

In that first meeting, we spoke at length about that awful American abstention. Every time I think about that vote, I don't just remember the embarrassing outcome, which America should have prevented. I also remember the sound of every other country's ambassador clapping, and the sight of Danny sitting there, alone in a room full of enemies and cowards. One of the first things I ever told him was that so long as I was ambassador, Israel would have a friend on the Security Council—and America would never abstain again.

There were many chances to prove it, but the biggest opportunity came less than a year into the job. It was 2017, and America had just made the long overdue decision to move our embassy to Jerusalem. The response was predictable. Country after country stood up to criticize us and Israel. One after another, the other fourteen countries on the Security Council voted to condemn America's action, and by extension, our ally Israel. But the measure failed because I vetoed it. It was one of the easiest and best votes I've ever made.

Danny and I worked closely in the buildup to that vote. We also coordinated when the embassy move came up in the General Assembly. Our efforts paid off. Normally, a vote involving Israel ends up with 10 percent or less of the world on the right side. This time, about a third of countries stood with us. In the messed-up world of the United Nations, that's a big win, and Danny Danon helped make it happen.

Our collaboration led to a lot of other wins for America and Israel. We worked together to rally opposition to Iran and the failed nuclear deal, get Arab countries to start paying more for Palestinian aid, advance a resolution recognizing Hamas as a terrorist organization, and call out the blatant anti-Semitism that characterizes so much of the UN's work.

One of our biggest joint focuses was reforming the absurdly named Human Rights Council. That organization has a standing agenda item on Israel, letting human rights abusers avoid criticism while attacking a democracy with an excellent record of protecting freedom. It quickly became clear that the Council wouldn't change its ugly, hypocritical ways. So Israel cut ties with it, and America withdrew completely.

My partnership with Danny led to a lot of good. And along the way, we developed a friendship that reflects the strong bond between our two countries. To me, becoming friends with Danny Danon was one of the best things that happened in my time at the UN. I learned a lot from him about Israel, her people, and her traditions. I traveled to Israel and joined him on a helicopter tour of the country. From that vantage point, he showed me a new perspective on Israel's struggle. We could essentially see the entire country, which is less than ten miles wide at its narrowest point. He fights as hard as he does because his country's survival demands nothing less.

Danny and his wife Talie were gracious to host me and my husband Michael for Shabbat dinner. We talked for hours about Israel's history, including the dangers it has faced and the courage of its people—a courage that has always enabled Israel to come through crisis stronger. It reminded me again why Danny did what he did at the United Nations. It isn't just a sense of duty that compelled him to serve. He is driven by a love of country, and so long as he lives, he'll do everything in his power to keep Israel safe.

There's no doubt Israel is stronger and more secure thanks to Danny's leadership. When I look back to my time at the United Nations, I count it a blessing to have worked so closely with him. But I also know that our work is far from over—and this book is proof of Danny's deep commitment to bring Israel higher. Both the threats and opportunities facing Israel are mounting, and its alliance with America is as valuable as ever for both of our countries. Danny Danon and I did our part at the UN to strengthen the bond between our countries. We will continue to build on that sturdy foundation.

Nikki Haley
U.S. Ambassador to the United Nations, 2017-19

CHAPTER ONE

Why a Strong Israel Matters

Israel is a beacon to the world.

When I first began to think about writing this book, the 2019 US election was being fought on the campaign trail, and elections were taking place in Israel. There were several political and social unknowns for the American people and for Israeli citizens. Both countries, and the world, were about to battle an unprecedented event: a global pandemic that took most of us by surprise. Because of my work at the United Nations, I was still living in New York in 2020 when the impact of COVID began to swirl around me. I was confident that my country would be on the front lines of medical research, vaccine development, and technology having to do with distance learning, health management, and security systems,[1] all vital to a post-COVID world. I wasn't wrong.

It became even more vital to outline my vision for a strong nation. *In the Lion's Den* is the result of that effort. We are a tiny country, but a mighty one. Like every other nation, we have the right to self-defense. We also have the obligation to continue to function as a strong democracy in a very challenging location of the world.

What you find in this book is a direct approach in describing the experiences I had over my five years of service at the UN and

1

in other public service realms as they relate to the future of Israel and its security. I don't hide or censor what I saw, heard, and did. In revealing these, I show what can and should be done regarding Israel's future. It is my roadmap for the hard and continuous work we need to be engaged in to ensure the safety and strength of my tiny nation in the middle of a tough neighborhood. While I write about the major highlights and historical moments that captured headlines, most of the things I accomplished were done behind the scenes—quietly and without fanfare or much international press. The idea of working for strength and security is found in a combination of many acts, large and small.

I believe my principles of global engagement, diplomacy, and foreign policy that you find in this book will guide Israel in a positive direction into the future. I share my experiences on the front lines of working for Israel's global presence for decades, including five intensive years at the UN. I share with you the moments of pride and success but also the disappointments and humiliations that have made me more determined. Entering the UN early in my career was also seen as unorthodox. Many of my predecessors arrived at the UN at the end of their political or diplomatic careers. That was not the case for me. I came to New York to work hard and lead change. I wanted to show what I believe is the path forward for a strong Israel on a world stage. The UN gave me that platform, and I am grateful for it. I demonstrated that my vision for Israel is the right one, and it can be realized with commitment and passion.

The Journey Begins

Forming a coalition government, one where a variety of political parties agree to unify and cooperate, is a complicated and sometimes lengthy process. Such was the case in 2015, when Prime Minister Benjamin Netanyahu worked for seven weeks to negotiate and solidify a majority in the Israeli parliament, the Knesset.[2]

He then had to decide on his own who he would assign to the top ministerial positions from his own party, the Likud. Tensions are high when you walk into the prime minister's office to discuss your future position. You don't really know how things will turn out, no matter what your aspirations may be. The prime minister has his own agenda, and it may not be the same as yours.

It was not the first time I was in this situation with Prime Minister Netanyahu; it was actually the third. The first time, when I was elected to the Knesset in 2009, I had no expectations in terms of becoming a minister in the government. I was thirty-eight, relatively young for a member of the Knesset. I became deputy speaker of the Knesset. Four years later, and more experienced in government and politics, I was also very popular within my party. As a result, I was placed in one of the top five positions in the party primaries, which indicated that Likud voters wanted me in a leadership position.

In that meeting, the prime minister told me that despite my popularity he could not nominate me as a minister because there were other, longer-serving members who would be upset to be bypassed. I did not buy this explanation, and I reminded him that when he was elected to chair the party at a relatively young age, he did not pay attention to similar sentiments. Ultimately, I accepted his offer to serve as Israel's deputy minister of defense, knowing that every day spent in this position would help in the future. I had no doubt that in the next government I would be on a shortlist of ministers.

After the 2015 campaign, the prime minister once again called the party leaders in to discuss the positions each of us would take. As I said, there is always anxiety surrounding the prime minister's dealings with the cabinet positions. It's never an easy process when several people are jockeying for the same handful of high-profile jobs. Even though Prime Minister Netanyahu had experience with making appointments, there were always surprises at the last minute, and usually at least one or two senior members would end up disappointed.

When it was my turn to discuss possibilities, I brought up my interest in dealing with some of the social problems in Israel, specifically as the minister of welfare. I was exposed to these challenges when I served in the Knesset as the chairman of the Committee of Immigration and Absorption. I felt that I could use my political power, energy, and leadership skills to help people who don't normally have a voice.

Prime Minister Netanyahu was surprised. He expected me to ask for a foreign affairs position and immediately told me that this position had already been promised to a colleague of mine who had years of experience dealing with welfare issues and unions. The prime minister had a different position in mind for me. He thought that because of my background and experience in the international arena, I may have an interest in heading an Israeli mission, but he did not indicate the location. We have dozens of diplomatic missions around the world so it could have been anywhere.

I humored him and said, "Why do you want to send me so far away from you?" He didn't laugh. He had more than a few political problems to solve before the swearing in of the new government that evening. He had a sixty-one-seat coalition in the Knesset, and he had to secure all the votes. I already knew that a few of my colleagues were not happy with the positions he had offered them; one even announced that he might not show up for the vote. Another was hospitalized a few hours before the voting would take place. I decided not to stretch his sense of humor and instead told him that the only diplomatic position I would consider would be representing Israel at the United Nations, but that I would also have to discuss it with my family. "Your family will thank you for the experience that you are giving them," he said, and he turned out to be right about that. In the meantime, we agreed that I would assume the role of minister of science and technology until I departed for the United Nations.

The next stage was to discuss the offer with my wife, Talie. She has long supported me in my political endeavors, but this time it was different. Moving to Manhattan would be a dramatic change for her and our three young children. We would have to leave our home in a moshav, a kind of Israeli agricultural community, which is surrounded by fields and greenery, for the skyscrapers and sidewalks of New York. I was sure it would be an interesting challenge. It was an opportunity to be in the frontline of Israel's foreign policy and to meet international players including heads of state. Mainly, I saw it as a chance to advance Israeli interests on the international stage, and address the seemingly intractable negative and often hostile view of Israel among some at the global body.

For my family, it was not an easy decision. It took some convincing on my part for Talie to see the possibilities of such a move. At that time, our son, Aviad, was fourteen and our daughters, Hila and Shira, were ten and eight years old. Talie and I discussed the challenges, including the language barrier and the unknowns of leaving behind the quiet life we had in Israel. To this point, I had been able to fulfill major public service roles while keeping my family outside of the heat of the political game; but now, it would be different. It would definitely change our lives in ways I could not begin to predict. The hardest part would be leaving my mother and Talie's parents behind. They were extremely connected to our children and deeply involved in their upbringing. Whenever I had to devote my time to political campaigns, they were so supportive. I thought that perhaps we should take them with us, but it was not an option. We knew that every Shabbat dinner without them, our kids would feel the loss. It would be a steep price to pay for the experience of living in New York.

We both understood that everything in life can change in a split second, so we decided not to discuss the idea with our children until we knew the UN appointment was a sure thing.

The prime minister is known for changing his mind at the last minute.

A week after the meeting with the prime minster, he sent an urgent request to see me. When I entered his office, he was sitting with his top advisor. In front of them was a copy of my first book *Israel: The Will to Prevail*. He started by saying that he was worried about the reaction of the Obama administration to my nomination. He wanted to be prepared for any push back from Washington. The prime minister had already taken a strong public stand against the Obama administration, so it wasn't as if my appointment to the UN ambassadorship would be surprising. I had included strong criticism of the administration in my first book, but it was reasoned and legitimate, particularly around the expectation that Israel would agree to a unilateral building freeze in Judea and Samaria.

The prime minister and his senior advisor went through the book meticulously to look at the points that they thought were problematic. Once they saw I did not use extreme language, and that my arguments were measured, we agreed that if there was any push back, we would have a well-prepared and coordinated response. When I left his office, I still felt that he was concerned about the reaction from the US to my nomination. However, I did feel secure that he would not change his mind about sending me to New York. I knew the prime minister very well; he is like this with every decision. Some may say he is an alarmist and a worrier, but I think it was always safer to be prepared for all possibilities.

Frankly, the prime minister felt that the UN was a good place for me, because he realized that I would be a thorn in the side of the more hostile contingencies there. He knew that I have no fear, that I do not give up, and that I have full command of the English language. He had also learned over the years that I was tough on ideological issues. He knew the UN very well, and he believed in my capabilities to make some headway with its attitudes toward Israel. Some argued that the prime minister was afraid of my popularity within the party ranks and wanted to remove me from the government. I will never know the exact reason he sent me, but I will always be grateful for the opportunity I received to represent my homeland and to lead Israel to many achievements in the international arena.

It was a Friday morning, and I was hiking in the Judean desert when the call came from the prime minister. He told me he wanted me to get ready and depart immediately before the opening of the general assembly. Once the appointment was announced, Talie and I knew we would have to hold a family meeting that same night. The reaction from the children was mixed. While they were excited to fly to the United States, I don't think they realized it would be a five-year stay. Shira, our youngest, was not excited about the idea at all. She kept arguing, saying, "It is your job so you should go by yourself, and I will stay in Israel with my grandparents." Despite the challenges, I feel it was the right decision for my family, as we became closer and overcame obstacles together.

The position at the UN gave me a chance to express my views regarding Israel, and why it must remain a strong and sovereign nation. Although some are skeptical about the UN's importance or effectiveness, I believe it is one of the essential platforms where we can make the case for Israel and ensure its productive, prosperous, and safe future. In order to accomplish this at the UN or anywhere, you have to be forthright—which I can say with confidence that I have proven.

There was an expectation that because of my background and strong ideological beliefs I would not fit into the world of diplomacy, that I was too much of a hawk and a "hardliner," which would make it difficult for me to build relationships and achieve anything of substance. That was the spirit of criticism in the press before I left Israel for New York—and there was plenty of it. *The Times of Israel* called my appointment "dismal"[3]; *Haaretz* explained there were six reasons to worry about me[4]; and the *Jerusalem Post* thought putting me in the post was the prime minister's way of thumbing his nose at the international community.[5] The American press was no less skeptical. *Bloomberg* took pains to describe the "odd" appointment,[6] and the *New York Times* expressed skepticism that a "right winger" could accomplish anything at Turtle Bay.[7]

To their credit, after winning many unprecedented achievements at the UN, some of the US media outlets that criticized me when I assumed the position apologized publicly about these initial judgments. However, my critics in the Israeli press were not as forthcoming; there were no apologies, and I didn't expect any.

How the Vision Formed

My views about foreign policy and the future of Israel that I present here have been refined by my experiences as a Zionist activist, member of the Knesset (the Israeli parliament), deputy minister of defense, minister in the government, and Israel's ambassador to the UN. However, my outlook was shaped well before my public service began, and it has only gotten stronger with time. I cannot separate my personal story from my political life; one informs the other. I was born in 1971, a tumultuous time for the state of Israel. The backdrop of my childhood in Ramat-Gan was loving at home but full of ongoing external conflicts.

My birth year saw the Palestine Liberation Organization (PLO) relocate to Lebanon, where it established a de facto state on its territory. This became a base for other international terror organizations. I was just a toddler in 1973 when the Yom Kippur War began. In 1975, the United Nations passed a resolution equating Zionism to racism. It was repealed in 1991, but it encouraged more hostility against Israel and its people.

Who would have thought that decades later, I would become a peaceful warrior for Zionism and for Israel, a beacon for democracy and liberty in the Middle East and for much of the world? My father, the late Joseph Danon, served in a special unit in the Israel

Defense Forces (IDF). As a reserved combat solider, he was called for duty every six months, including during the Six-Day War and the War of Attrition, which occurred between 1967 and 1970. Israel experienced a very intense period after the Six-Day War, when terrorists infiltrated Israel from Jordan. My father was only twenty-nine when he had to leave his young family and the electrical business that he had just opened to join his friends in one of Israel's best reconnaissance units.

During a fight in the Jordan Valley with terrorists who were heading to commit a terror attack in a civilian community, my father sustained a severe head wound. It resulted in lifelong hardships, including complete hearing loss and several challenging physical issues. Yet he was a fighter; he was devoted to Israel's cause. Because of his passion for the country, which I witnessed on a daily basis, I was filled with the same love and an understanding of why a strong and safe Israel is so important for the future of the Jewish people. This idea has gone through periods of erosion, and often seems to prevail today.

In my eyes, the story of my father, Joseph, represents the story of our nation and how it was built. It serves as a very important context for my views about foreign policy as it relates to our security. My father was born in Alexandria, Egypt in 1940 to a traditional Jewish family with Zionist sympathies. The idea of moving to Israel was always in their minds, but only after the establishment of the state of Israel did it become a reality. Even before the gates of Israel were open to Jews from Egypt, my family had already dreamed of that moment. My father's paternal uncle, Ovadia Danon, was very involved in the Zionist activities in Egypt, which was considered illegal at the time and dangerous. He was the first to go to a university in Cairo and was the first in the family to serve the intelligence services of the young Jewish state.

After the establishment of the state of Israel, it had become harder for my family to live in Egypt, as the atmosphere toward Jews had altered and had become hostile. Overnight, the appeal of Alexandria as a cosmopolitan city changed. The open, vibrant atmosphere had now become toxic. The colorful Jewish community life changed to fear, and everyone was looking for a way out. There were few options for the Jews who wanted to relocate. For my grandparents, there was only one option: Israel. Despite the letters they received from relatives in Israel who described the hardships newcomers would face in this young nation, they did not hesitate for a minute. They turned down offers to relocate to France and started to plan their journey to Israel.

In order to get to Israel, my father's family took a boat from Egypt to Italy. My father's nickname was Jojo. He was the first-born and just ten years old. From the day he left Egypt, he felt he had to provide for and help his family. The boat they boarded was headed to Brindisi, Italy to a transfer camp. On the boat, his family met a couple from Italy who had no children. They offered to adopt little Jojo because he was a nice-looking boy with a friendly personality. He didn't know if it was a serious offer or not, but it made a lasting impression on him, nonetheless. He answered loudly to the Italian couple that the only country he would go to was Israel, and that he had a mission to help his family.

My grandfather had worked at a successful printing company in Egypt, and my grandparents had to leave their property and memories behind, along with many friends. They had only their suitcases. The willingness to take the risk and leave everything behind demonstrates how important reconnecting to the Jewish homeland was to my grandparents and for so many other Jews who made the journey. The family had wanted to leave before 1948, but it was impossible at the time. Before the establishment of the state of Israel, the British Mandate restricted immigration to Israel.

There was much passion, excitement, and romance about moving to Israel. In practical terms, it was difficult. The reality is that in its beginning stages, Israel was a poor country that was trying to absorb hundreds of thousands of impoverished Jews over several years. Upon arrival, my father's family joined other families in a temporary relocation camp—basically refugee camps with hundreds of tents in the middle of nowhere where they waited in difficult conditions to be sent on to a permanent location. For someone who had come from Alexandria, a sophisticated, cosmopolitan city with every imaginable amenity, it was a culture shock. It was not easy to leave prosperity and familiarity for a complete unknown.

On the one hand, the physical downgrade was hard. There was no water or electricity. Living in a tent after coming from a house with everything including household help definitely challenged the spiritual elation they felt. My father told me he helped his father assemble the tent that would become their home and how they used all the skills they could to keep it from falling down when the rain and wind came. Everything was done in that tent, including cooking, studying, eating, and sleeping.

From there, they were sent to a permanent location that was not much better. They were transferred to Or-Yehuda, a small town near Tel Aviv, where they also lived in a tent until they were able to move into a small wooden shack with a metal roof and a dirt floor. Outhouses served as the family bathroom. Summers were hot and winters cold. My father came of age in this one-room shack, where sleeping, studying, and cooking were performed. Despite the poverty, they were grateful to take part in the miracle of establishing a Jewish homeland. Joseph found a group of new immigrants from Turkey who became his best friends. He loved to study and read, and to travel around the country. Because of his family's hardship, he had to drop out of school at sixteen in order to get a job and help the family financially. He loved school, but it was a luxury in such circumstances. Despite this, he continued to read everything he could get his hands on and traveled everywhere he could. His next opportunity was in the military, where he became one of the best navigators in an elite infantry unit.

Once Joseph joined the military, he met people his age from different parts of Israel; the Israeli military is a real melting pot.

He was placed in a special reconnaissance unit, where many of the commanders were from the Kibbutzim sector of Israel, or a collective community. One weekend, one of his commanders gave him a ride home in a military jeep to Or-Yehuda. What he saw—the shacks and the conditions my father and his family lived in—was shocking. That people still lived this way in Israel came as a surprise to the commander. Even though it was the 1960s, these enclaves still existed. My family was modest and worked hard to make a living. Only years later did they receive public housing in a nearby location.

The shacks have long been demolished, but the public housing is still there. My father and his siblings joined the military, studied, and built beautiful families. Despite the hardship and unpleasant conditions, they remained optimistic and focused on the future, rather than dwelling on present difficulties or sorrows of the past.

I have taken my children to visit the places where my father grew up. I remember his recollection of a warm and happy house, but when my children looked at it, they could not imagine living in such a tiny apartment, with a miniscule kitchen and one bedroom for a family of seven. My grandparents' generation overcame numerous challenges, fueled by their jubilation at the opportunity to serve and build their homeland with other Jews.

I was very close to my father and often acted as his translator and interpreter, his ears and his voice, when we went out and about. Consequently, we spent a great deal of time together. There are two fundamental truths I learned from him, which continue to inspire and influence my vision for Israel today.

The first was the importance of understanding our connection to the land of Israel. It is not just enough to know the history of a place; I cannot overstate the importance of that knowledge. Your knowledge, your roots, and your connection to a place are deepened when you know its topography. Despite his severe disability, my father was able to help me learn about Israel's regions, trails, backroads, and archeological sites. At approximately eight thousand square miles, the geography of Israel is diverse, and it includes desert conditions in the south and a snow-capped mountain in the north. My father made it a point to understand Israel by walking the land, our true homeland, and passing this knowledge to me. Before his military injury, he was able to travel extensively. He came to know the land very well. He would explore every valley and mountain north to south. His military service was intense; he would walk hundreds of miles each week.

After his injury, when he could no longer hike, I took many hikes on my own, enjoying the beauty of the land. When I returned from each excursion, I would describe to my father what I did and saw. It was a way for us to connect even though he could not travel with me. We could reflect together on the experience of the hike. I was his eyes and his feet. He would listen and share new ways I could make a trek the next time. By the time I was twelve or thirteen, I knew almost as much about the land and the stories connected with it as he did. As a result, I didn't need a GPS to find my way around the country, whether on a roadway or a trail. Knowing the land has strengthened my commitment to preserving what is ours.

The second fundamental lesson was the ability to take a stand. My father gave me the confidence to speak out. He advised me never to be shy about expressing my thoughts or commitments. My father overcame many obstacles, including the reaction of other people when they saw him after his war injuries. Because he was physically hurt in the war, and could not speak well or hear, he had to deal with miscommunications and misunderstandings on a regular basis. I often acted as translator for him because he could not hear anything and could not conduct conventional conversation. I spoke to him very slowly, and he would read my lips. I would walk with him to banks and other offices, and speak on his behalf so he could understand what was happening. This gave me the confidence to speak, ask questions, and argue if needed.

He could have decided to stay home and hide, but he did not. Even so, he tried to keep busy and work whenever his medical condition allowed. One vivid memory is the time he put an ad in a newspaper as an electrician. After his mandatory military service, and a few years before his wartime injury, he opened his own company for industrial electricity. The company was very successful, and he had won a lucrative contract for a few buildings shortly before he was called back into service and injured. When he recovered enough to come home, he was sure that he still had the basic skills to do simple electricity work. But he had suffered neurological injuries, which affected his ability to work.

One day, I received a call to fix an electrical problem. He said he wanted to give it a try. I accompanied him to a house in the neighborhood, carrying his tool box. He did a terrible job; the entire house lost power. Instead of feeling ashamed of him, I felt quite proud that he tried to make a go of it. He didn't do it for money, but just to be busy and contribute. Seeing this and other valiant efforts my father made in an attempt to be useful had a profound effect on my own character. It contributed to the strong feelings I have today about Israel's place in the world.

As a result, I am not afraid of what people think of my views, words, and actions, nor am I reticent to express them. Thanks to my father, I have a strong work ethic and inner convictions that give me strength and stamina to push my ideas. This makes me a strong adversary when necessary. If you have something to say, just say it, he would tell me. If I believed in an idea, I should not be shy about sharing it, nor should I be intimidated by bullies or those louder or more popular. Weak ideas are fleeting; strong ideas are eternal.

Going Forward

How does this translate to my vision of Israel today? In terms of dealing with hostile actors and rogue nations I, like many Israelis, have embraced the warrior mentality of both my father and heroes like Menachem Begin, the first prime minister to sign a peace treaty with an Arab country.

Israel's foreign policy has a long history for a relatively young country. It was shaped over a period of at least one hundred years before the establishment of the state in 1948, and has continuously centered around maintaining autonomy and independence in the region and the world. How those key goals are executed, achieved, and maintained has differed depending on the leadership and other stakeholders, but the seven key principles remain constant: (1) creating and sustaining a Jewish territory with a significant Jewish population; (2) developing a robust and self-sustaining economy; (3) finding and maintaining strategic alliances and support of global players and nations who share our values; (4) evolving a "never again syndrome," meaning that Jews would never again find themselves unable to defend themselves against hostile actors; (5) creating an evolving defense doctrine that is based on our unique geography in comparison to the region it's in, with the aid of a committed people's army; (6) ensuring access to necessities like water, food, and fuel to sustain the well-being of the state; and (7) reaching out to our neighbors as potential partners when possible and as a way to neutralize regional threats.

This book lays out the ways we can achieve these goals. These include being proud of our heritage; never apologizing for who we are as a people; using technology and innovation to build bridges and help others; maintaining a position of active engagement worldwide; using the tools we have, while looking for and developing new ones; and working directly with a variety of countries and individuals to build fruitful relationships, to open minds, and to shift negative opinion.

My vision is defined by my own pillars as a public servant, activist, and diplomat. In order to achieve or influence others, you must build knowledge and awareness one step at a time. The mosaic is created over time, through hundreds of meetings and phone calls, getting to know people, building confidence, and helping others. Whether it is facilitating the move of embassies to Jerusalem or other victories, many important breakthroughs begin quietly, behind closed doors.

There are many reasons for everyone to care about the future of Israel. Aside from biblical or religious reasons centered around our presence in the Holy Land, which is important to the major religions of the world, Israel acts as an example of the strength and the value of democracy in a region where it is in short supply. The reality and challenges of what is on our doorstep and how we respond to it is a case study for those who face radicals on the ground and in the cyber world. These kinds of attacks started against Israel but rolled onto the shores of other democracies. Even our fiercest critics admit that Israelis know more about mitigating and defending against all forms of threats than anyone else on Earth.

Israel offers incalculable strategic value to larger democracies, because we maintain more enviable technologies and human-intelligence capabilities than any other country in the Middle East. We have a strong understanding of our neighbors as well as the threats around us, and we willingly share our knowledge and understanding. We know how to deal with our neighbors both good and bad, we can collaborate with and warn those at risk, and defend against those who seek to harm us. For example, we learned about an attack planned for an Australian aircraft thousands of miles away, and that information helped thwart what could have been a devastating loss of life. This is just one instance where our intelligence has prevented terrorism.

Israel has committed on-duty soldiers in its military who are on the frontline of defense of our nation. We also have triple the number of reservists, citizens who leave their homes and families to voluntarily heed the call to protect the nation whenever required. We can mobilize this people's army rapidly.

Our knowledge of preventing war and fighting when there is no other choice is unsurpassed. We act to prevent extreme situations in areas on the border where enemy capabilities and violence are a problem. We monitor our borders and protect our civilians from the enemy proxies who threaten us from the north and the south.

We continue to try to open the eyes of the international community about a nuclear Iran. While we do it diplomatically, we also prepare our military at the same time for a scenario that would make it necessary to prevent Iran from obtaining a nuclear bomb.

Our innovation and creativity go far beyond defense technology. Despite being approximately the size of New Jersey, a citizenry of less than nine million people[8], and with almost no real natural resources, Israel has the third-most companies listed on the Nasdaq Stock Market, after the United States and China. We are second to none when it comes to technological talent, demonstrated by the fact that many of the biggest high-tech companies in the US, including Google and Intel, have created research and development facilities in Israel. When I took on the challenge to represent Israel, I knew that once I could show people what we have built in a short period of time, it would change their perception of us completely.

Israelis use modern technologies to revolutionize existing industries and create entirely new ones based on a variety of evolving global needs. Through its own boldness and entrepreneurial spirit, Israel has become a renowned global leader in industries ranging from high technology and agriculture to manufacturing and tourism. Cutting-edge Israeli institutions such as the Volcani Institute produce a staggering 75 percent of all agricultural innovation. Israel's growth rate consistently outperforms bigger developed nations; its per-capita capital investment is two and a half times bigger than the US, and eighty times China's.

All of this is to say that Israel and its ideals, its principles and vast intellectual resources, created in a very short period from next to nothing as my family's story attests, are worth preserving, growing, and emulating. I share my story and its crucial moments in this book because this is what has helped set my vision for Israel's future, a vision I will continue to actively pursue in any way that I can, through writing, activism, and public service.

This book shares how I was able to transfer the Israeli experience to other people through hundreds of engagements. Not all of them were successful, but this is an ongoing process.

There are times when leaders have to make hard choices, not because of short-term political, economic, or social gains, but simply because it is the right thing to do. Leaders involved in policymaking should not be distracted by the passing parade of the new or popular. I will never forget the day when a UN Security Council's resolution to condemn Israel was passed in December 2016, at the bitter end of the Obama administration. The US did not veto the resolution, which had been its response to such UN resolutions in the past, but instead let it stand. Shameful. The lesson for me was clear: Israel must stay its course, remain committed to its principles and goals, stand sovereign and autonomous, and understand that this setback was not the end of a journey— but a bump in the road.

Although I was in a public position that allowed me to meet hundreds of people, the UN is also a diplomatic battleground where I felt alone most of the time. Despite the friends Israel makes, the allies it builds, at the end of the day, Israel is also alone. We must make sure we have the capacity to defend ourselves; it is not enough to depend on our strongest allies. I was able to build bridges, create coalitions, and win important seats of influence at the UN. You always have to count only on yourself. It may seem like a contradiction, but it is a truth I must emphasize. I memorized the last words Elie Wiesel, of blessed memory, once said to me after one meeting: "Always pay more attention to the threats of your enemies than the promises of your allies."

This moment and others like it brought me back to the values my father instilled in me in childhood about faith, persistence, and trust in myself. There are three crucial memories that support the values I bring to my public service. The first are the stories that my father told me about his childhood as an immigrant in a new land. No hardship I would endure would come close to the experience of building a new life from scratch.

The second is a desire to reach out, build bridges, and make friends. In the early sixties, after his military service, my father traveled the world, including through various parts of Europe. He made many friends wherever he went. Hearing about this gave me the same urge to travel and learn about other places and cultures, and to reach out a hand of friendship whenever and wherever possible. Third, his injury had a profound effect on me and my ability to overcome hardship. Obviously, I saw the consequences firsthand, every day, as I helped my father navigate the world. He never complained or had any regrets. Given the chance, he would serve again, even with the knowledge that he would be severely injured.

No matter the outcome of battles along the way, a vision for the future of Israel must be an engaged and active one. Even when you have a difficult moment or reach an impasse or a deadlock, you can overcome these with your strength of convictions and proactive and responsive responses. Foreign policy is not only done in the halls of the UN or in the Knesset, or with leaders of foreign nations in their lavish offices or diplomatic headquarters, but in everyday ways and in a variety of situations. The future of Israel depends on an active policy that is expressed and embraced at every opportunity. The case for a strong Israel must be made consistently in a real and personal way. When you look at the long run, persistence and resolve is key. This book shows how Israel can stay the course and secure its place in the world, and explains what it has and can achieve with such an approach.

CHAPTER TWO

A Victory Mindset

We must be in the arena to win.

The foundation of a successful foreign policy is a victory mindset—to view all challenges and obstacles with a can-do attitude and that nothing is impossible. As the first prime minister of Israel, David Ben-Gurion, once said, "In Israel, to be a realist, you have to believe in miracles."[9] History shows us that decisions must be made from this point of view where the challenges are many and constant in the quest for peace and security. Sir Winston Churchill, Britain's wartime prime minister, used the victory mindset as a successful platform. As soon as he was appointed, he shared his "no surrender" approach.

On October 29, 1941, after he had left office, he was asked to deliver a commencement speech to students at the Harrow School, a college preparatory institution. This speech was brief and to the point, and it included these iconic lines: "Never give in. Never give in. Never, never, never, never—in nothing, great or small, large or petty—never give in, except to convictions of honor and good sense. Never yield to force. Never yield to the apparently overwhelming might of the enemy."[10] This is the very essence of a victory mindset. We do not give up because it's too hard to continue, we do not give in because it looks to be an easier route, and we do not give over, because we never get anything but more strife in return.

Many events, achievements, disappointments, and moments of great emotion, both joyful and heartbreaking, occurred during my five years of service as Israel's official permanent representative to the UN, or as it is usually referred to, as Israel's ambassador to the UN. When I took the job, I knew it would not be permanent for me, even though the job felt never-ending in terms of the challenges and attacks I faced in that role. There were also positives and progress, including several firsts that conventional wisdom said would be impossible. I was elected chairman of the UN Legal Committee, becoming the first Israeli to chair a committee since my country joined the international body in 1949. I brought Judaism to the UN in unprecedented ways, including facilitating the inclusion of kosher food in the UN cafeteria, recognizing and celebrating Jewish holidays, and promoting and encouraging the purchase of Israeli innovations and products by the UN itself. Visiting Arab countries in my official capacity as a UN ambassador was remarkable both from a historical perspective and a personal one. Although the visits were conducted under secrecy and tight security, they were a success and enabled us to build new bridges and foster understanding.

These are not minor accomplishments when you consider that the UN is an institution that has long been predisposed to hostility toward Israel. They also signify what I believe should be an important goal of foreign policy and global engagement, which is to use every existing tool and venue to forward the interests of Israel and to demonstrate that what is good for Israel is good for the world. This is the only way Israel can move successfully into the future, no matter the winds and whims of global politics and policy. We should be steadfast.

The secret to decisive leadership on the path to a strong Israel often means tossing out conventional rules. It means remaining optimistic when optimism seems to be in short supply. It requires you to put your head up, look adversaries in the eye, and face head-on conflicts and mindsets that seem fixed. It is not easy; however, the alternative, allowing others to control the narrative while you try to keep up with ephemeral political fashion, which makes your efforts more difficult and less effective.

After serving five years in the most intense and demanding position in the Israeli diplomatic world, working with two American administrations and three US ambassadors at the UN, I found myself in extraordinary situations, interacting with superpowers and world leaders, seeing both their weaknesses and their moments of glory. I saw firsthand issues of enormous global interest but also smaller human moments, which, in many ways, are more telling and informative when we think about the future of Israel. We need to thrive in a very tough neighborhood, win even in an uncompromising place like the UN and with diplomats from unfriendly nations, and communicate directly with a huge variety of people from the public and private sectors who represent diverse ideas.

The right to live and prosper on our land is a constant in my resolve to secure Israel's future, as it should be for anyone fighting for the same goal. Any future thinking about Israel must be grounded in winning victories big and small, and remaining unhindered by losses on the way to our goals. I learned this fortitude from my father, who never wavered or felt disappointed because of his own hardships and the injuries he sustained while fighting for Israel. In my house, the most important day of the year was Yom HaZikaron or Memorial Day for Israel's fallen soldiers and victims of terror. It is a significant day for me, and it was always an emotional one for my father. He was not capable of listening to the news coverage of related events on that day because his injuries had left him deaf. Nevertheless, he was glued to the television, watching the ceremonies and reading the names of fallen men and women as they scrolled across the screen.

I never quite knew if he was so moved because of the friends he lost, and he had lost many, or because of his own wounds and the personal price he paid. It was likely a combination of both. In many ways, his life stopped at the age of twenty-nine when a grenade blew up next to his head. That moment, when he was evacuated from the Jordan Valley in a helicopter to Hadassah hospital in Jerusalem, he also lost his past life. Yet he had always stressed that we should be willing to pay any price for our independence. I had no idea just how significant and powerful this sentiment would be during my service at the UN.

The Stage Is Set

The story of UN Resolution 2334 sets the stage for this overarching idea. New York was sunny but cold and crisp on Friday, December 22, 2016. Since it was so close to Christmas Eve, many UN ambassadors had already flown back to their home countries to enjoy time off with their families. My family was looking forward to a hard-earned break. Winter in New York seemed cold and bleak to my children—very different from the blue skies and warmth that was so familiar to them in Israel. We looked forward to leaving Manhattan to spend a few sunny days in Puerto Rico for Hanukkah. I had scheduled a Shabbat dinner for my family with the Chabad rabbi of the island, Rabbi Mendel Zarchi. Everything was organized, and we were excited to get going. Once we touched down on the island and it was okay to turn on our cell phones, I saw a text message from a diplomatic colleague of mine from one of the Muslim countries asking me to call him. *ASAP*.

After I disembarked, I immediately called him from the airline gate. He told me that the US and other countries had decided to present an anti-Israel resolution in the UN Security Council. I assumed, as the final language had not been settled, that the resolution would include a strong declaration condemning the presence of Jewish communities in Judea and Samaria, and Jerusalem.

This would become Resolution 2334, which also contained language that asserted Israel was violating international law.

There had been talks in the corridors of the UN that President Barack Obama wanted the resolution crafted and voted on before he left office. The end of his term was now less than a month away. We thought we had gotten a pass, and that he had changed his mind. I had hoped his thinking would be stronger than his emotions, but it was not the case. He wanted to conclude his term with a UN resolution that would define the legacy of his Middle East policy.

The November 2016 US election was over. It was clear that the new administration under President-elect Donald Trump would not support such a condemnation. Then Secretary of State John Kerry and President Obama were working diligently behind the scenes to make the Resolution and its passage a reality before they left office. This was very bad news. Once I hung up, I called senior diplomats to get more information, including ambassadors to the security council, to ask if they had heard about it.

The world of diplomacy and foreign policy makes for interesting friendships. Other ambassadors with whom I was close didn't call me to reveal Obama's plan. Only one, a Muslim, shared the news with me. Other ambassadors were asked to keep it quiet, but once I called them, they couldn't lie. Of course, they admitted they knew about the resolution. I had a thousand things I had to do, sorting them in my head as I worked, including updating the prime minister and telling my family that I had to go back to New York, but that they could stay in the sun for a few days. I bought a return ticket at the gate. When I reentered the plane, the flight attendant asked if I had forgotten something. I said no, I have to go back to New York.

If not stopped, the resolution would go to the floor the next day, December 23rd. Time was of the essence, because supporters of the resolution, including the US, EU, and the Palestinians, wanted to put the resolution to a vote on the Friday before the official close for Christmas. I made an all-out effort to call every-one possible who I thought could thwart it. I knew it would be an ugly battle. Usually, the US works with us against such initiatives; this time, however, it was the US pushing the resolution. The only thing we had in our basket was that in two weeks a new adminis-tration would arrive in Washington. President-elect Trump spoke out, making it clear he was against the resolution; any countries friendly to the US must decide carefully which side to take.

Prime Minister Netanyahu was in Israel doing his part to try and stop the vote. His efforts to talk to President Obama were futile, as the president was apparently unavailable. The official excuse was that he was already on Christmas holiday in Hawaii and couldn't take a call, which was disingenuous. The fact that the strongest ally of Israel was avoiding a call from the prime min-ister made me realize I was on my own. At that point, the prime minister was skeptical that speaking with the US Ambassador to the UN, Samantha Power, would do much good. He didn't think I'd make any headway with her, as he felt strongly that President Obama was committed to allowing the resolution to pass. Still, I tried. Unfortunately, the prime minister was right. My efforts to reach Power before the vote were unsuccessful. It was frustrating. Power and I had worked together very well up until this point. We had enjoyed an open and honest dialogue, and now she was refusing to take my calls, which was a red flag. It was calculated and strategic on her part. Ignoring my phone call showed just how strained US-Israeli relations were at that moment.

I talked to some of President Obama's close friends. These sup-porters tried to convince the president and others in his adminis-tration to change their minds about the resolution, but they were unsuccessful. The prime minister believed the resolution was the result of a personal grudge President Obama had against him, rather than a political strategy. After all, it's not as if the resolution would improve prospects for peace in the region or better the lives of the Palestinians. It would do neither. The prime minister had delivered a powerful speech in the US Congress in March 2015 against the Obama administration's Iran deal.[11] I have no doubt that this angered President Obama. The US backing of the resolution was his administration's parting shot. Ultimately, the US facilitation of the resolution's passage did not support the peace process and only hurt President Obama's legacy.

I shifted my strategy from trying to change the president's mind to trying to change the mind of other countries on the security council a few hours before the vote, which was scheduled for mid-day. I had to convince them to either reject the resolution or at least abstain. At that time, Egypt was a member of the security council representing the Arab League. It had co-sponsored the resolution. However, due to pressure from the incoming Trump administration, Egypt withdrew sponsorship. That was meaningful despite knowing that Egypt would ultimately vote in favor of the resolution. At least its name wasn't on it.

Once Egypt pulled its sponsorship, we thought it might be possible to delay the vote into the next US administration. We felt that if we could at least push the vote until after Christmas, it would be too late for the outgoing administration to put it forward. Of course, both sides were playing for time. For the resolution's supporters, it was full-steam ahead to get it presented and passed before Christmas. At that moment, everyone was pressuring the resolution sponsors who remained—New Zealand and Senegal.

I gave the prime minister credit. When he has a task to complete, he is like a man obsessed. He tried to speak with the leaders from the two countries. Despite the issues with time differences, he kept pushing. "Wake them up," he said. It was easier said than done. It was 1 p.m. in New York and 6 a.m. in New Zealand. Still, the New Zealand ambassador was not eager to make such an early call to his prime minister, Sir William English. I spoke with Prime Minister Netanyahu many times on this day. His instructions were unequivocal. He asked me to convey a definitive message to New Zealand and Senegal: If they continued their sponsorship of the resolution, we would close our embassies in Wellington and Dakar, and cut our diplomatic ties with them completely. I used strong language with both countries' ambassadors, even though it created a temporary diplomatic crisis with them. We weren't playing around.

There was controversy about New Zealand's support for the resolution before and after the vote. According to reports, Minister of Foreign Affairs Murray McCully hadn't received the country's cabinet approval to sponsor the resolution. That could mean there was a chance they would withdraw support, but it was not to be. For New Zealand, it was about feeling relevant and important. The ambassador was excited about the chance to promote a security council resolution that concerned the Middle East.

In one of our meetings, I nearly lost my temper. I asked him if he really understood the importance of Jerusalem to the Jewish people, to the people in Israel, and it was apparent, looking at his face, that he hadn't a clue. I advised him to speak to his colleagues at New Zealand's embassy in Israel, and I was amazed when he told me that New Zealand didn't have an embassy in Israel. He explained that their embassy in Turkey "covered" Israel. I thought to myself, what the hell does New Zealand have to do with our issues? Unfortunately, this was not the first time I identified the desire of some countries to try to become relevant at Israel's expense.

We had a strong bilateral relationship with Senegal, and we knew the country was being used against us by more powerful nations. We knew that France in particular was pushing Senegal behind the scenes to sponsor the resolution. But it was too late. It refused to withdraw support. Ultimately, New Zealand and Senegal became the resolution's front men, pawns used by the US, France, and the Palestinians.

Ukraine also wanted to abstain, but they didn't. Ukraine is very friendly to Israel. During its term on the security council, Ukraine helped us many times. I have a strong friendship with

Ambassador Vladimir Yalchenco, who is now the ambassador to Washington. But the country was in an impossible situation. It was getting pressure from three different directions: Obama, the incoming president, and Israel. At the end, they decided to support the resolution, because they were afraid that President Obama would take measures, even at the eleventh hour of his administration, to hurt them.

As far as the UK, I personally feel we missed an opportunity. Prime Minister Theresa May had just been elected. I learned two months after the vote that she was seriously considering abstaining or even vetoing the resolution. This was extraordinary because the UK generally follows the European Union's (EU) positions, which are generally pro-Palestinian and anti-Israel. Had I known about her thought process sooner, I would have put more effort into mobilizing or influencing May on this specific vote. I found out that she actually considered vetoing the resolution in order to signal the president-elect that she is interested in forging a stronger partnership with the US. In the end, pressure from the foreign office was stronger than May expected. We had limited time and energy. Looking back, if we had been informed in advance and had more time to plan, we might have been able to change the result.

This turn of events was unprecedented in the history of US-Israeli relations. We understood this was not going to be good for us. This was, in short, a hostile diplomatic attack against Israel pushed through in the final days of the Obama administration. It has also become one of the more unfortunate legacies of the US administration, at least in terms of international relations.

For Israel, the most crucial aspect of these events was the lack of communication with the US administration before the vote. It meant there would be no coordination with our strongest and most powerful ally—obviously the US didn't want to coordinate any aspect of this vote with Israel. They wanted the resolution to pass. For the first time in decades, the US and Israel were working against each other on the floor of the UN.

The wording I would use in the debate and what we would say after the vote had been fine-tuned. I was ready for all scenarios.

The day had come. From the moment I landed in New York until the next morning, I felt as if we were conducting a battle, a diplomatic battle. I prepared myself for the vote, and the numbers of who would vote for or abstain looked quite bad. I decided that after the vote I would go out to the media and thank President Obama if he decided to veto the resolution. The more likely scenario was that the US would abandon us. The real decision was how to respond if they failed to veto the resolution. I made the personal decision to go on the offense against the US and its secretary of state to expose what they had done if they did not veto this resolution. This brought out my background as a warrior—when you get punched, you defend yourself, you don't go to the corner and stay silent.

In the morning, we called anyone we could. I understood I had done whatever I could, and it was not enough. This was a time of great emotion and reflection for me. Some events are beyond our control, but we have to deal with outcomes in the best way possible. I had to remind myself that this vote would not change the lives of Israelis or Palestinians in the short term. I even had a sense of optimism that the new administration would undo some, but not all, of the damage that would be done.

I still could not get in touch with Samantha Power. In my experience of public life, if you don't get an answer, it's a bad sign. I prepared two speeches, one in case I was wrong and the resolution was vetoed by the US. In this optimistic scenario, I would talk about the bond between America and Israel, our shared values, and the need for direct negotiations. I always go back to examples of the peace we achieved with Egypt and Jordan—not through the UN Security Council, but through strong leaders negotiating directly.

There are times when you have to say something with dignity but with strength and without reservation. I had a feeling that the second version of the speech was the one I would deliver. I am a realist. It had been prepared in the event that the resolution passed. In it, I exposed the US abstention for what it was: a shameful and pointless maneuver against Israel. I had an important point to make and wanted the US administration to feel uncomfortable. Why should I make it easy for the administration after they abandoned Israel?

I also stressed that the resolution was an empty victory for the Palestinians and would benefit no one in the region. They would not be encouraged to go back to negotiations but would continue to look to the UN for meaningless answers. In my speech I reminded the council that in a few weeks there would be a new US president, another policy, and a new era.

Several hours before the vote would take place, I had a marathon of meetings with strategic ambassadors at the UN, including members of the security council. I met with the Russian ambassador, the late Vitaly Ivanovich Churkin, knowing he wasn't comfortable with the Obama administration's initiatives at the security council. There was a very slim chance he would use Russia's veto power to block the resolution, even though historically Russia had always supported the Palestinians. An experienced diplomat with many years at the UN, he could perhaps be able to persuade Russia to block the resolution or maybe delay it. In the past, we didn't agree on many things, but we were friendly and had a productive relationship.

After our meeting, I felt he was less comfortable with the resolution and especially with its timing. He promised to speak to Moscow immediately. Churkin made a few phone calls, and we met again after a few hours. He told me that because of Russia's commitment to the Palestinian cause, he could not veto the resolution, but he was not happy about it either.

When I told him I had to rush to another meeting, Churkin had one last thing to tell me. He revealed an important piece of information. Apparently, Obama and Kerry had facilitated two resolutions regarding Israel. The first was Resolution 2334, which we knew about. The second resolution was called Parameters for Peace. It was never discussed or publicized. It outlined President Obama's vision for peace in the Middle East, which set certain parameters for an agreement between Israelis and Palestinians including borders, refugees, and the status of Jerusalem. Churkin told me that the Russians would veto Parameters for Peace if it came to a vote. While Russia realized that both resolutions were pointless, it would not veto the first one, but Russia also didn't want to give Obama a parting gift by allowing the second one to pass. I believed him, because I knew Russia did not want to help Obama. Churkin didn't like either of the resolutions, but the Parameters for Peace went very far against Israel. Russia minimized the damage by blocking it. Had the resolution been blocked by a Russian veto, it would have been quite embarrassing for the US.

I thanked Churkin, and on my way out of his impressive office, I asked him to do his best to postpone the remaining resolution. After getting in my car in front of the Russian embassy, I asked my staff, my security detail, and my driver to stand outside while I updated the prime minister. I told him about the second resolution and that I was sure it would not come to a vote because the US would not give the Russians an opportunity to veto it and in doing so embarrass and upstage them.

Right before the vote, we entered the packed security council hall. Live streaming equipment had been set up to show the proceedings around the world, in real time. Ambassador Churkin surprised everyone by asking for a closed consultation of the security council before the vote. All fifteen ambassadors went into a side room, where Churkin tried to postpone the vote. He could not go against the resolution directly; instead, he said he wanted to hear if any of the member states wanted to discuss the resolution before the vote. It was Friday afternoon, 1 p.m. If one country said it needed more time, he could have pushed the vote from Friday until after the weekend. That would have been very good for us. This is something I appreciated, because I knew it was hard for him to do. Unfortunately, the US, the Europeans, and the Arab League were eager for the vote to take place immediately. They demanded to go back to the hall and put it to a vote. After what seemed like ages, the fifteen ambassadors emerged from the side room.

Once they came back, Samantha Power asked to speak to me in one of the consultation rooms. This was after I had tried to call her many times. When I entered the room, I knew exactly what was going on. She told me that "the president decided the US would abstain. It's unfortunate this is about to happen, and I'm sorry." I was unmoved by her apology. "It's unfortunate that no one will remember all the good things we did together over the years. The legacy of the administration in terms of US-Israeli relations will be captured in this shameful moment," I told her. And that was exactly the case. We made advancements at the UN with the Obama administration, but no one remembers them.

Obama had played a very tricky game. If you support the resolution, if you helped craft its language, why not take ownership of it? And why not vote for it? By abstaining, the US pretended to be neutral, but it was in the middle of it. It was dishonest to abstain. Frankly, I would have appreciated it if the US would have taken the stand publicly that they took behind closed doors. The administration was actively engaged in negotiating and drafting the language of the resolution. Why not be honest and transparent about it and tell the American and Israeli people what it was doing? Israel knew what was going on. Shouldn't the American people and the world know as well?

To be clear, the resolution itself was not a direct product of the US or designed or written directly by the president and his staff. It came from a combination of countries unfriendly to Israel at that time and on this issue, including Sweden and France. However, during a series of closed-door meetings and maneuvers, President Obama and his team were instrumental and engaged in crafting how the resolution was worded and what would happen when it came up for a vote. The US did not consult Israel about the resolution on any level, which was also unusual, because in the past we would be at least told about similar developments and initiatives. On the contrary, they purposefully kept us out of the game.

We could have argued or debated had we been included, but we had no chance. It was done behind our backs. The US enabled the push for the resolution in the council quietly but powerfully. They used proxies to push their agenda, and it was cowardly to do so. I knew all of this, but there was still hope in my mind about whether or not the US would veto the resolution, as they had forty-two times in the past, including in 2011 when a similar resolution had come to the floor.

I walked back from the consultation room and took my seat in the security council. I greeted my fellow ambassadors and found the strength to joke with them. I hid my emotions and made a joke with some of my colleagues, saying I hoped we wouldn't be in the room past Christmas. A few of them whispered that they were embarrassed that they had to vote against Israel. My face was expressionless, I wanted to make sure no one saw how I was feeling inside. While sitting with colleagues as part of the security council, and in front of all the representatives of almost the entire world, along with numerous television cameras and journalists, I felt in my bones what it meant to be alone in the lion's den.

At that moment, I felt for the first time the meaning of the words in the Bible, that the people of Israel will be alone among the nations. Every move I made, every expression, was being recorded. I needed to gather all the strength and power I had. I remembered my father telling me that Israel is our land and we have no other place in the world. It gave me the strength and inspiration to remain calm and focused. I texted the prime minister confirming that the US would abstain while shielding my phone from cameras that could focus on it and share my private communication with the world.

Then, I watched my worst fear realized. Resolution 2334 was approved with fourteen member states voting in favor, the US abstaining, and no votes against it. A US veto was not forthcoming.

For the Palestinians, it was a celebratory occasion. The minute it passed, the Palestinians in the hall were clapping and cheering. After all, it was a victory for them. For them, to embarrass and condemn Israel at the same time was a great achievement.

Alone in a Crowd

Right after the vote, everyone stood up. I was the only one sitting in the room while people clapped and hugged each other. I thought, what is this celebration about? It's not going to help the Palestinians or the peace process. I also felt the strength, conviction, and values of the message I was about to present. The president of the security council gave me the floor, and I delivered my speech[12]. I looked each ambassador in the eyes before starting my speech. I proudly mentioned the times in history that were difficult for us but that we overcame—the Babylonians, the Romans. "We will also overcome this shameful resolution," I said, "and no resolution will remove us from Jerusalem." The room was packed with Palestinian supporters because they knew, like I did, that the resolution would pass, and it would not be vetoed. That meant I was by myself when I gave that speech. In the long run, I said, we will prevail. No one can change history, the history of Israel.

I looked at Power and told her that within a few weeks there would be another ambassador sitting in her chair and another president in the White House who would go back to the policy that represents American support for Israel. Little did I know that one year later, I would sit in the same chair and discuss the historical decision of the US to move the embassy to Jerusalem.

What unfolded next was a rush by the US to justify its actions. Looking back, I am reminded of being bullied along with some of my classmates in grade school. My father encouraged me to stand by my principles. If someone started to berate, belittle, or beat on me, I had to give it back, even if he was older and stronger. The other kids in my grade would not respond if they were punched or shoved, but the older children knew if they did it to me, I would fight back without hesitation. One day, I came back with bruises all over my face and body. My mother asked me what happened, and when I explained that an older kid was pushing and shoving, she was worried, but she also praised me for standing up and fighting back. After a few more incidents, they stopped bothering me. This memory reminded me that you often have to stand up for yourself, by yourself, against stronger players. Now, I was facing a public confrontation with the major superpower in the world. Sitting idly by was not an option. I kept my cool as I moved to the next round after the vote, revealing to the world what role the US had played in this disgraceful moment.

I would not give it a pass, and we would not go quietly. The fight had just begun. I was not intimidated by President Obama or John Kerry. I immediately booked as many media interviews as I could. I began to set Israel's public response, and I did not ask permission to reveal what the US had done behind the scenes, because it needed to be exposed. I would not allow the US to claim that it had nothing to do with the resolution to go unanswered. My actions forced the US to justify itself and take some heat for its actions. This is a model for what should be a crucial part of Israeli foreign policy. Do not back down, always expose wrongdoing, and force those responsible for it to explain themselves in public.

In this case, the public approach was necessary since the US was not speaking to Israel directly. The media became our go-between. I led the attack on the senseless and dangerous resolution and the shameful cowardly behavior of the US administration. I said it out loud to the media that the US chose not to stand with its closest ally. One of the first interviews I gave was to CNN, telling the anchor John Berman that the US had acted shamefully. He was incredulous and asked how I could use such language. I said there was no other way to describe it. I went on many more American TV news shows to explain what happened, and I always used the same strong language.

It was not easy or pleasant, but I had to stand my ground. I stressed in more than a dozen interviews that the vote and the US's reaction to it was shameful and deeply regrettable. For me, it was a real change of attitude. We, the US and Israel, were no longer there to fight together against extremist factions from Iran, Hezbollah, or Hamas. Rather, we were fighting with each other. It was a low moment in US-Israeli relations, but I knew it was temporary.

I found myself in an adversarial situation with John Kerry, the US Secretary of State. I don't think Kerry was expecting a strong reaction from me or from Israel, as he was very bold in criticizing us. It became a game of ping pong. He was sent by the US administration to defend the resolution. It didn't make any sense. On the one hand, the administration was saying they had abstained from voting and that they had nothing to do with drafting the resolution. On the other hand, instead of staying low key, they sent the secretary of state to every news studio possible to brag about the importance of the vote.

Kerry's words were confrontational. He defended the decision to abstain, explaining that "it was for Israel." He held a special press conference where he focused on Israel's human rights violations, including emphasizing the idea that the Jewish communities in Judea and Samaria made the situation more volatile and peace talks more tenuous. He questioned the strength of our democracy. This was ironic given that he knew very well that Israel is the only place in the Middle East that is a socially liberal and open democracy, with much economic freedom, and a high tolerance for diversity. Minorities in Israel participate in our vigorous democracy, are elected to parliament, have served as ministers, and preside at all levels of our judicial system, including the Supreme Court. I only wish secretary Kerry had put the same passionate effort into other events during his tenure.

The war in Afghanistan was then the most lethal conflict in the world. The conflict in Syria and Yemen have had the highest number of organized political violence compared to other nations around the world. Syria was, and remains, the deadliest place for civilians, and a major humanitarian crisis. The Philippines was a war zone with more civilian fatalities in some recent years than in Iraq and Somalia. And yet the UN's obsession with Israel took precedence in its halls and was now being encouraged by the US.

The president knew the resolution would not benefit the Palestinians, nor would it result in any dialogue between the Israelis and Palestinians. If you want to promote peace, you can't get there with a resolution at the UN. President Obama said this himself at the UN, in 2011, when he gave a speech to world leaders[13]. He said, "There is no short cut to the end of a conflict that has endured for decades. Peace is hard work. Peace will not come through statements and resolutions at the United Nations.... Ultimately, it is the Israelis and the Palestinians who must live side by side. Ultimately, it is Israelis and Palestinians—not us—who must reach agreement on the issues that divide them: on borders and security, on refugees and Jerusalem."

I agree with President Obama's own words from 2011, when he noted that to achieve peace, you have to enter into direct dialogue. Allowing the Palestinians empty victories in the halls of the UN reduces the chances of having meaningful, productive, and direct dialogue. The resolution would not and did not change Israel's commitment and obligation to protect its people while pursuing genuine peace. In fact, looking back at what happened since the vote, there is a general agreement that the resolution didn't improve the lives of Palestinians on the ground. The Obama administration's invisible facilitation and support of the resolution was its last attempt at payback.

And then that administration and its policies were gone. Nikki Haley was nominated as the US Ambassador to the UN. I had the honor to accompany Ambassador Haley on her first visit to Israel shortly after she was confirmed, and from there, we forged an alliance and a friendship. More good news was forthcoming.

The Embassy Moves

On December 6, 2017, the Trump administration formally stated that the American embassy would be moved from Tel Aviv to Jerusalem, and in doing so, would recognize Jerusalem as the capital of Israel. This was something that the US Congress had approved many years ago. The law said the embassy would move, but it also gave the president an option of signing a waiver every year. All the previous presidents had signed the waiver even though they said they would not. President Trump did not sign the waiver, and he actually moved the embassy.

Many presidents had made similar commitments during elections, but ultimately, they were never fulfilled. In 1992, President Bill Clinton said "Jerusalem is still the capital of Israel and must remain an undivided city accessible to all." In 2000, President George W. Bush said, "As soon as I take office, I will begin the process of moving the United States embassy to the city Israel has chosen as its capital." Bush added that he would "start the process as soon as I'm sworn in." It never happened. Even President Obama said in 2008, "Jerusalem will remain the capital of Israel, and it must remain undivided."

Some of the promises to recognize Jerusalem as Israel's capital may have been sincere. Some were made for political gain. So, it's not that all of these politicians were lying. Pressure and threats from others scared them away from acting on what is absolutely a bold decision.

President Trump made the promise and delivered on it. In fact, Trump wanted to announce on his first day of office that he would not sign the waiver and that the embassy would be moved. I had received a phone call from a friend who was involved with the Trump transition team who revealed the idea of declaring the embassy move on his first day in office and having a ceremony at the White House. The administration was putting a list of invitees together, and my friend wanted me to look at it to ensure no one was omitted. This was a sign that the administration was serious; it wasn't just a campaign promise, to be forgotten. Trump was actually going to implement it.

The announcement and event did not happen, of course. While President Trump made a commitment to declare the embassy move on his first day in office, once he started to receive pressure from some US agencies and important players in Jerusalem, he postponed the declaration. However, the president did keep his word. On December 6, 2017, he announced the United States' recognition of Jerusalem as the capital of Israel and ordered the planning of the relocation of the US Embassy from Tel Aviv to Jerusalem.

I knew about the announcement ahead of time. Ambassador Nikki Haley and I had been working together and had established a strong relationship. She had a successful visit to Israel, and we had built mutual trust. She had seen firsthand the complexities and challenges of Middle East policy and practice. We scheduled a phone call to discuss the implications of the announcement, knowing it would create an outcry from certain factions. I did something I usually don't do because I am so focused on tasks. I told her, before we talk about the technical details, let's take a moment to appreciate that we are taking part in a historical moment. This was something that our children and their children will read about in history books, and here we are preparing the groundwork. It was a unique honor to be involved in the move. She was very excited and told me it was an honor to be serving her nation in this way.

Both of us knew there would be a debate in the security council. We strategized what would happen at the UN when the announcement was made by the president and when the inevitable vote condemning it came to the floor.

The security council vote came after powerful speeches by Nikki Haley and myself. In her speech, Haley accurately described the near obsessive level of anti-Israel sentiment and action at the UN. "The United States will not be told by any country where we can put our embassy," she said.[14] She was proud of the president's decision, honored to be the only voice of support in the security council, and took satisfaction in vetoing the resolution condemning it. It was a historical and emotional moment when she raised her hand and used her veto power to stop the resolution from moving forward.

My speech stressed the centuries-long historical connection of Jews to Jerusalem. "When it comes to Jerusalem, we do not back down," I said. "Some 3,000 years ago, King David declared the city of Jerusalem to be the capital of the Jewish people. Our nation has never given up when faced with an adversary. We will not allow others, including the United Nations, to determine our fate, in particular when it comes to Jerusalem: not then and not now."

Right after the vote, when the security council meeting concluded, I approached Ambassador Haley. I thanked her for her speech but told her that this would not be the end. Knowing the players on the other side, I had no doubt that the resolution would make its way to the general assembly. There, resolutions have more of a declarative meaning, and while they are less powerful, there is no veto power over them.

As I had envisioned, the Palestinians approached the GA with a push to condemn the US decision to move the embassy. We had one day to prepare for the debate, and it was important that I convey to the world the importance of Jerusalem to the Jewish people. There would be less than ten minutes to make my case, so I had to do something memorable. I called a dear friend of mine, David Bari, affectionately known as Davidala, the founder of the City of David Expeditions in Jerusalem. I have known Davidala for almost thirty years, from the time he started excavations in the City of David[15]. I told him about the UN debate and asked him to send me an important artifact or symbol, something tangible, that could prove the connection between the Jewish people and Jerusalem.

Davidala knew someone who would be traveling to New York on the day of the speech, and he gave that individual a valuable coin from the Great Revolt, minted in the old city of Jerusalem in 67 A.D. The coin dates back to the second year of the Great Revolt, when the Jews rebelled against the Roman Empire, a pivotal moment in world history. One side of the coin reads, in Hebrew, "Freedom of Zion," and the other reads, "Year two of the revolt."

The plan was that while I showed the original coin from the podium, interns from our mission would give each ambassador a replica of the coin accompanied by a short, written explanation about it. Before taking the podium, my chief of staff approached me to tell me that the UN ushers informed him that protocol banned us from distributing anything during my speech. "Today, we fight for Jerusalem, and we don't follow protocol," I told him as I walked to the podium of the general assembly. In the middle of my speech, I slowly took the tiny coin out of my pocket and aimed it at the camera as I spoke. I was nervous not to lose the coin, as I knew how important it was. As planned, while I presented the ancient coin, my staff swarmed the general assembly and gave each ambassador the replica. I told the hall that the coin proved the connection of the Jewish people to Jerusalem, and that this connection is unbreakable. "No General Assembly resolution will ever drive us from Jerusalem," I said. It didn't change the vote, but seeing and touching the coin helped people understand our emotions regarding the eternal connection between the Jewish people and Jerusalem.

I was sure that the coin would be the highlight of the speech, but the media actually picked up on a strong line I used to describe the general assembly's automatic support for any anti-Israel resolution. "Those who support today's resolution are like puppets. You are like puppets pulled by your Palestinian masters." I called the vote itself, "nothing more than a performance of delusion." Before the speech, some of the diplomats in my mission had advised me to remove these lines from the speech because it might offend some in the general assembly, but I refused. When people deny our connection to Jerusalem, it is a direct insult to our core values. My colleagues were shocked, but with all due respect, it was my speech. When you have people voting against something without considering the language and history, you must point it out. Once I saw the ambassadors squirming in their chairs, I knew keeping the language in was the right decision.

As we expected, the United Nations General Assembly voted by a huge majority to reject the US recognition of Jerusalem as the capital of Israel. We worked to get as many countries to abstain or vote with us in the general assembly as we could, but only the United States, Israel, and seven other countries voted against the resolution[16]. Several countries abstained[17]. Other ambassadors simply left the room. Despite the fact that every country has the right to decide where to place its foreign embassies, 128 members voted to condemn the US decision to move its embassy, and in doing so, challenged or doubted our historical connection to Jerusalem.

Ambassador Haley was irritated to see the pattern of votes and acted on the spot by immediately extending an invitation for a winter party at her residence to the countries who stood with the US. The minute I received the invitation, I told my wife we had to postpone our plans so we could attend. It was a great decision on Haley's part. Even though we lost the vote and were supposed to be embarrassed about it, we celebrated with the many countries who in their own way had rejected the vote. It was jubilant, like a holiday party, since it was right before Christmas. I will never forget the look on the faces of some European ambassadors who were not invited to the party—shock. They asked me why they had not been invited, and I happily explained to them the reason. It was evident that they were not happy to be snubbed from social events.

Despite the vote in the general assembly, its timing could not have been better—almost exactly a year from the day the UN voted to denounce Israel's presence in Jerusalem, our ancient capital. The US officially recognized Jerusalem as the capital of Israel, vowed to move the embassy and, in May of 2017, did just that.

On May 14, 2018, the US embassy officially opened. A ceremony took place in Jerusalem, but both Ambassador Haley and I decided to stay in New York. It was a festive and deeply symbolic moment. Jerusalem was covered with US and Israel flags. Many Americans had traveled to Israel, both Jewish and Evangelicals delegations. I wanted to be part of it, but I knew that my duty was to stay at the UN. Nikki and I scheduled to meet in the US mission in New York at the same time the ceremony in Jerusalem would be taking place. When I walked into her office, I saw a bottle of champagne. I don't drink during the day, but on this occasion, I made an exception and savored the moment. Together, we toasted the opening of the embassy.

Unfortunately, the intelligence community had advised us that the Palestinians were planning major riots ahead of the opening. I wasn't surprised; I knew from experience that the Palestinian leadership would do everything they could to destroy any celebratory occasions for Israel. The terror group Hamas mobilized tens of thousands of people to riot at the border fence with Gaza. It was not a genuine protest. Some were carrying guns and explosives. Many used children as human shields. The goal was to break the fence, infiltrate Israel, and allow terrorists to go inside and attack our communities.

The order to our soldiers was to minimize casualties but not allow them to bring the fence down and cross the border. Coverage of the opening ceremony of the embassy was tainted by this violent activity. Many news stations had split screens, showing live coverage of both the opening ceremony and the violence at the border. Some news outlets ignored the opening and focused only on the riots instead because it was not a peaceful protest. We were forced to defend our people and tried to minimize the casualties. We did block the massive riots, and although tens of thousands were mobilized to break the fence, it was not breached. Still, Hamas was successful in disrupting the festivities, and fifty-eight casualties were reported[18].

Doomsday predictions that claimed the move would inflame the entire Middle East never materialized. The embassy welcomes more than one hundred American diplomats to work each day, who work closely with Jews, Muslims, and Christians, on a variety of diplomatic and commercial issues. International tourists visit every day. We have put to rest the myth that recognizing Jerusalem as the Israeli capital would spark broad and bloody violence in the Arab world. It sparked no violence anywhere, except for a short-lived, orchestrated violence financed by the Hamas terrorist organization.

This did not come as a surprise to me. "Jerusalem is an inseparable part of Israel and her eternal capital. No United Nations vote can alter that historic fact." This quote comes from a statement by Israel's first prime minister, David Ben-Gurion, spoken on December 5, 1949, just days after the UN voted for a resolution calling for the internationalization of Jerusalem. Indeed, the embassy move turned out to provoke very little controversy as had long been feared. And for many people including myself, the move holds a powerful symbolic significance.

Back then, Ben-Gurion's response was to move forward with a planned announcement about the moving of our parliament, the Knesset, and other national institutions to Jerusalem. The announcement by the Israeli government was met with condemnations from around the world. Even the US refused to hold any diplomatic meetings in Jerusalem, and they continued to send official cables to an office of our foreign ministry in Tel Aviv. Nevertheless, Ben-Gurion's brave decision was the right one for the future of Israel. It made clear the idea that turning our historic capital into an international zone administered by others was a nonstarter for Israel and that Israel would not shy away from making the right decisions no matter what kind of international pressure was placed upon us. We are deeply and historically connected to our capital; we are not foreigners, crusaders, or colonizers.

Finally, and probably most importantly, the decision to move the embassy can, and I believe already has, set in motion events that will make peace between Israelis and Palestinians more likely. Guatemala and Honduras have also moved embassies to Jerusalem, which I discuss in more detail further on in the book. Israel exists in a tough neighborhood where strength is respected and perceived weakness can lead to violence. Israel is here to stay, and no amount of war or military might can defeat or remove us. The recognition of Jerusalem as our capital can serve as a healthy reality check for the Palestinians. As more countries recognize our capital as fully under Israeli sovereignty, the reality will set in that neither terrorism nor UN Security Council resolutions will succeed in forcing our hand on a compromise in Jerusalem.

Freed from at least one part of the Palestinian's unrealistic expectations, these new developments may encourage them to finally turn to sincere and direct negotiations. There is a high price that the Palestinians will pay for continuing the conflict and perpetuating the violence. They do not improve or preserve their position by remaining unwilling to make peace and clinging to the false dream of eliminating Israel.

As I write, there is a new administration in the White House, and with it, new policies toward Israel. It matters what they are, of course, and it may necessitate changes to our diplomatic approach and how we negotiate our policy. But what can never change are our values and eternal connection to our land and to our united capital.

CHAPTER THREE

Never Hide, or Apologize

Being honest about who we are and what we
believe takes us further than denying or hiding it.

I've never shied away from expressing my personal or professional convictions, especially in public service. It has served
me well, and I believe it is a strategy that serves Israel's global
standing effectively.

The idea that in diplomacy you avoid directness is not my philosophy. I believe in telling the truth. When I was disappointed in
countries and peoples, I would tell them directly. When it came
to a point where one would apply a double standard regarding our
right to self-defense, blaming Israel for using "disproportionate
force," I would expose my critics for what they were. Hypocrites.
When the French ambassador would begin to criticize our security
forces for the way they reacted to riots, I immediately reminded
him how rioters were treated on the streets of Paris. During a
violent demonstration in France by a social protest group called
The Yellow Vests[19], the French police used whatever means were
at their disposal to stop the unrest. No one complained about an
excessive use of force by French police; no one on the security
council demanded an urgent meeting about it.

I pointed this out to the French ambassador in a public meeting of the security council. While he did not appreciate it, he no longer brought up the claim of excessive or disproportionate measures when discussing Israel's right to defend itself since that incident. He knew it would not go unnoticed. Many countries in the UN disapprove of intervention on domestic issues, but when it comes to Israel defending itself, it becomes a topic for international discussion, including how we fight terrorism. We have an obligation not to stay quiet about it. Whenever they bring up the way we defend ourselves, we should remind them of how other democracies act when they are under attack.

I came to this point of view from an early age, on the heels of my father, which I have discussed. I also grew up in the Betar movement, an organization founded in 1923 in Riga, Latvia by Vladimir (Ze'ev) Jabotinsky. This is a Zionist youth movement that believes in the cause of a homeland for the Jewish people and national pride. Chapters quickly sprang up all over Europe, including during World War II. Betar was a major source of recruits for Jewish regiments that fought the Nazis alongside the British. Betar volunteers played vital roles in independently resisting Nazi forces and their assaults on European Jewish communities.

Betar graduates played a prominent role in the underground movements that were integral to the fight for the establishment of the Jewish State. Once the British mandate was over and Israel was established, the Betar youth movement continued to be a successful incubator for conservative Zionist leaders. Dozens of leaders, including Menachem Begin and Yitzhak Shamir, started their political career in the youth movement. It will always be my honor to serve in such a unique environment.

July 21, 2020 marked eighty years since the passing of Vladimir (Ze'ev) Jabotinsky. His main message was "Silence is filth," as in you shouldn't be quiet about your convictions and when you see wrongdoing. At the very beginning of my tenure at the UN, it was difficult for me to set aside this philosophy and maintain diplomatic protocols. However, I quickly realized there was a way to both speak my mind and maintain expected professional etiquette. The two are not mutually exclusive. It is imperative that we do not live under the weight of silence for fear of offending someone with our truth.

Indeed, those who are reticent to talk about their identity and beliefs in the mistaken notion that doing so will hurt someone's feelings or create a situation where progress cannot be made are operating under a critical misconception. From a strategic point of view, any kind of fear, including fear of being honest about who you are and what you think, is noticeable and seen as a point of weakness that your adversaries can and will exploit. From a personal point of view, I don't want to live my life tiptoeing around because I'm constantly worried about who I might offend. That is not the example I want to set for my children or my constituents. I am a proud Zionist and committed to my values.

One place where this kind of honesty and transparency has served Israel well is at the UN. It's one of the most challenging environments for us, made more so by those who want to apologize for being Jewish, Israeli, or Zionist, or at least keep these facts under wraps or minimize them. It has shown me that our future can and will be more secure if we are openly authentic about our national identity.

What many people don't understand is that there is a public UN and a private UN. The public face of the UN—at least when it comes to Israel—is aggressive and bullying. But privately, you can build bridges, forge friendships, and create a space for understanding, particularly if you are transparent.

I took it upon myself to foster as many friendships with fellow ambassadors as possible, including those from Muslim countries. In terms of national security, this bridge building is imperative. Today, many of these ambassadors are very close to me, and I consider them allies. I have visited a handful of Muslim countries with whom at that time Israel had not yet established diplomatic relations. These trips were productive because we have more in common than we have differences. The one issue about which we all worry is the challenge of dealing with radical Islam. As a result of this mutual interest, we have cooperated with each other to block Iranian hostility in the region.

Indeed, most of the Arab ambassadors with whom I have built relations have a genuine curiosity and interest in Israel. In many cases, they admire us, in large part because we have not backed down from our positions, we have built an amazing nation, and we are an unapologetic Jewish state. When I discuss the Middle East with these men and women, they tell me they appreciate what we have achieved in a short period of time. I believe it's only a matter of time until we will be able to publicly expose the cooperation between Israel and those moderate Arab countries—but only if we continue a policy of standing tall for who we are.

The Lessons of History

My conviction to wear my identity on my sleeve is rooted in my background and a personal history shaded by both conflict and a deeply rooted love for my country. Standing at the UN at the podium for the first time as Israel's ambassador on October 22, 2015 was an emotional moment for me. Dozens of cameras, ambassadors from all over the world, and people from everywhere were watching me on television and online. According to protocol, before reaching the stage at the general assembly, you must sit by yourself with a UN representative nearby. It was just me and my speech at that moment. Once I took the podium, I understood I was not representing myself; I was speaking on behalf of my country, on behalf of fourteen million Jews from all over the world. No one could tell but it did take me a minute to gain full control of the situation while maintaining my composure. I have delivered hundreds of speeches in my life, including hundreds at the UN; but that first one at the UN, I will never forget.

I thought about my father. He was no longer with me, not able to see his youngest son standing in the lion's den, in front of all the nations of the world. It was a very proud moment for me, and I knew my father was with me in spirit. Everything he had taught me came with me to that podium. His struggles, wounds, and passion filled me as I spoke for the first time. It was also an opportunity to set an expectation for how I believed we should communicate as a strategic part of policymaking.

Many people were surprised at my forthrightness, and others were dismayed. Some editorial writers from the left, and so-called experts, lamented my appointment specifically because they knew I would not hide or cower. I read one Israeli analyst note that my appointment amounted to a "cruel joke" on the international community. The new envoy "lacks even the slightest level of finesse and subtlety required of a senior diplomat."[20] The Israel-based British writer Jonathan Cook wrote that my appointment was "part of a discernible pattern of recent appointments by Netanyahu that reflect a growing refusal to engage in any kind of recognizable diplomacy. Confrontation is preferred."[21] They were proved quite wrong, as I demonstrate in this book.

The speech I gave to the UN that day was not what I had envisioned as my first address. However, in the six weeks prior to my first public appearance at the UN, the streets of Israel had been swept by a savage tide of terror, which pundits and politicians called a "cycle of violence," which implies a back and forth between equal factions, which was not the case. In my speech, I made one thing clear—the attacks on innocent Israeli citizens did not represent a cycle of violence. I reject that assessment. They were only unprovoked attacks against Israelis for no reason other than the fact that they are Jews living in their historic homeland. Like any country, I continued, Israel has the right and obligation to defend its citizens, and this is exactly what we are doing and what we will continue to do. Any country whose people are being attacked in the streets on a daily basis would act in the exact same way. There is no equal side in a situation where terrorists attack a sovereign democracy.

An example is a thirteen-year-old boy who leaves his house with a kitchen knife intending to kill someone, and then chases and stabs an Israeli boy riding a bicycle fifteen times[22]. This radicalism comes from the indoctrination of a culture of hate. Nelson Mandela once said, "No one is born hating another person.... People must learn to hate." Tragically, Palestinian children have been receiving lessons in hatred from their leaders, in their schools, and on children's television programs for decades. I described the kind of "education" Palestinian children receive—not math or reading, but hatred of Jews. The Palestinian representative sat with his chin in his hand, stony-faced. I do not think he expected me to give such a speech, but he listened.

Another influential figure in my view of Israel's future and how policy should be shaped is Yitzhak Shamir, the seventh prime minister of Israel, who served two terms during the 1980s. He had been an influential leader in the underground, part of one of its most militant factions, the Lehi, in the 1940s. Shamir wasn't particularly charismatic and is not considered as one of Israel's most well-known prime ministers. His commitment to Israel came directly from his convictions, which he pronounced with pride. He was one of the most important leaders in modern Jewish history.

For me, Shamir was one of the most important role models in terms of critical policy decision-making, which served Israel well internationally and domestically. His leadership serves as an example of the kind of strategic strength that unapologetic convictions bring. Shamir faced criticism from many Israeli leaders, pre-independence, who were more interested in British approval than the national and legal rights of Jews. During his days as prime minister, Shamir cemented the unapologetic approach of an independent Jewish nation with full control of our destiny.

In terms of Israel's long-term viability, prosperity, and security, Shamir was able to win a major concession from the US when in 1991 he convinced President George H. W. Bush to stop steering Soviet Jewish émigrés away from Israel and toward the US. The majority of Russian Jews sought asylum in the US after first passing through a European country. From there, they were granted asylum in the US. Shamir claimed it was not acceptable, because the Jews don't need to seek asylum; they have a place to go, their homeland, Israel. That argument convinced the administration. The Soviet Jewish diaspora that followed fundamentally transformed Israel's economy and improved its strategic position in the region.

Shamir didn't worry about being liked. He was certainly not particularly popular with the US government or European leaders. But they respected him. By standing up for his identity as a proud Jew, and for his country, he earned Israel the respect of the world, even if it was grudging. No matter; it made a difference in the nation's ability to negotiate with other countries with equal footing. For example, during his tenure, important countries including China and India renewed diplomatic relations with Israel.

In 1993, after completing my military service at the rank of lieutenant, I traveled around South America with a limited budget of $1500. With a backpack and a small Hebrew-Spanish dictionary in my pocket, I visited Brazil, Bolivia, Peru, Ecuador, Colombia, and Venezuela, learning Spanish along the way. This opened my eyes to many cultural experiences. Since that time, I have been eager to build friendships with as many individuals from around the world as I can.

Afterward, I served as an emissary for the Jewish Agency for Israel in Florida, promoting Zionism among Jewish students. As part of that effort, I organized an event for Prime Minister Shamir to speak in front of about a thousand Jewish students. It was a great experience for me, as it was my first public event that I organized as a civilian. During mandatory military service, you have to present your leadership skills in many circumstances. But this was a different ballgame. Here I had to coordinate everything from scratch, there was no existing infrastructure on which to depend on. Coordinating the visit of the Prime Minister, fundraising for the first time in my life, recruiting students to attend this mega-event, and most importantly, preparing a speech in English, were challenges I took on with gusto. It was a one-man show, I had no staff to help me and only a few excited and motivated volunteers.

Two days before the event, I realized that I didn't have a proper suit. When I arrived at the local Macy's in Aventura Mall, I realized that even the most basic navy-blue suit cost nearly $200, an amount I could not afford at the time. While I was asking the salesman about more affordable options, I saw a sign that explained the store's return policy. For someone who had just arrived to the US, I was happy to learn that I could receive a full refund within fourteen days of purchase. That was amazing for me. I bought the suit, and during the entire event, I made sure not to get close to anyone holding food or drink. I knew that I could not return the suit if it showed any signs of wear, so I took very good care of it before bringing it back shortly after the event. I was relieved when Macy's accepted the return.

The event was amazing. The prime minister, who had just completed his term, was very open and direct. When one of the students from the University of Miami asked him about the demographic challenges with the Arab Israelis, Shamir looked at the young student and told him, "Don't you worry, young man. We will bring more than one million new immigrants from the Soviet Union in the near future." At that time, it sounded like the wishful thinking of a former prime minister, but Shamir had seen the realization of a few remarkable visions during his fascinating life. In 2000, more than one million new immigrants did indeed come to Israel from the former Soviet Union.

The event gave me great confidence for the future, mine and Israel's. I realized that with the right message, you could accomplish many things and motivate people to take action even if they weren't wearing uniforms or getting paid. After the event, I had dinner with Shamir, which gave me a chance to talk to him one on one. As a child, I read every book I could find about the Jewish resistance movements. I asked him what gave him the strength to fight the British Mandate and push the British out of Palestine while he was simultaneously leading the underground. Shamir told me about three pillars of wisdom that I continue to cherish and use today. The first pillar is ideology, what you believe. The second pillar is choosing the right organization, the vehicle you use to promote those beliefs. The third and most important is persistence. This is where most people fail. His recipe for success sustained me in all my public service work. PM Shamir was the last leader who truly believed in this three-pronged approach. After he finished his term in 1992, the discussion and paradigm for peace changed. Prime Minister Shamir was the last leader in Israel who did not care about his image or legacy but only about doing what is right for the Jewish people.

Starting in 1993, a few leaders adopted a policy of appeasement, that is, to give something to our enemies in the hopes they will leave us alone. In 2005, Prime Minister Ariel Sharon removed every Israeli housing development and soldier from Gaza[23]. Did it result in peace? No, in fact, it allowed Hamas to seize power two years later, sparking numerous conflicts. Thousands of rockets and hundreds of attacks from Gaza have been launched, resulting in hundreds of civilian casualties. The appeasement strategy exemplifies the dangers of staying silent or reticent about your ideals in the face of wrongdoing, bullying, and violence.

As a result of the guidance of the important influences in my life, and my own convictions, I never hide my devotion to Judaism. I believe this is an important aspect of Israeli foreign policy and a source of Israel's strength. Those who oppose your goals can detect those who hide from who they are. They can easily identify this as a point of weakness. My pride for Judaism was never opaque. I put it on the front page. I did the opposite of what too many people do when they are in similar political situations, when secularism is thought to rule the day. I read from the Bible in official speeches and other events and celebrated Jewish events and holidays at the UN. I brought Judaism to the UN's front door and inside its halls.

By bringing Jewish holidays to the UN, the religious experience and ceremonies we performed inside the UN made them real and accessible to others. I recall one Hanukkah event early in my tenure, with many dignitaries including Israeli President Reuven "Ruvi" Rivlin and major philanthropists. It was suggested that along with traditional Hanukkah songs we also sing Christmas carols—but this was not a Christmas party. This was unacceptable for me; I did not want Christmas songs to be sung during a Jewish holiday that celebrated our independence. While I enjoy participating in Christmas parties, this was a Hanukkah party. I made it clear that this would not happen during my tenure, and it didn't.

Ultimately, these events increase understanding. The reality of Israel and Judaism was also strengthened in more than a hundred ambassadors' minds when I hosted their visits to Israel in a variety of delegations or missions. This combination was a winning strategy. I also found I could learn from some of the ambassadors, who were devoted Christians who knew the stories of the Old Testament better than many Israelis—some quoted passages they knew by heart. This experience was humbling and gratifying.

The idea for the missions was hard to implement at first. Many of the ambassadors who were initially invited to join me in Israel were afraid of the pushback and criticism they would receive once they returned to New York. Convincing them otherwise required effort and many personal meetings on my part. After the first group returned from visiting and shared their experience with colleagues, the attitudes of skeptics changed. In fact, I quickly started receiving requests to join future trips and even complaints from some at not being invited soon enough. I also received unexpected support from the Palestinian representative, who wrote a letter to the capitals of all the missions who came with me, complaining that they had made such a trip. If one thing ambassadors do not like, it is when someone complains about them in their own capitals. The representative's behavior created resentment among many ambassadors. So while he hoped to stop the missions with his letters, they did exactly the opposite. Missions increased.

This initiative proved to be a great investment of my time. I saw the results in the change in attitude toward Israel in the general assembly. Many of the ambassadors who made the trip were later promoted to ministers of foreign affairs, and in those positions, they continue to remind me of the great experience they had in Israel. In some instances, I receive requests from ministers to participate instead of ambassadors, and my response is always that everyone is invited. If you want to come, we welcome you. Seeing is believing—showing people the country is the best way to explain Israel. I will always commit to that idea.

The ambassador to the UN from Antigua and Barbuda, Walton Alfonso Webson, who is blind, visited Israel with me. For him, touching, not seeing, was believing. I usually take ambassadors to the historic tunnels that brought water to the City of David. This time, I took Ambassador Webson to the Pilgrimage Road, the thoroughfare used to make the pilgrimage to the Temple Mount. Now it is open to the public, in the City of David, and visitors can walk on the same stones as ancient peoples did. Our visitors could feel the walls and hear the sounds in the underground system. During that trip, we stopped in a place where an ancient coin is stuck into the ground. We showed this to the ambassadors and enabled Ambassador Webson to experience it by giving him an actual coin to sit and examine with his hands. After a while, he told me, "Now I feel the connection of the Jewish people to this land."

Some may say that Antigua and Barbuda and other similarly small countries are insignificant to international relations and the work done at the UN, so why bother with their ambassadors? This attitude is wrongheaded and shortsighted. All countries can play a part in changing attitudes that go directly to policy, especially at the UN, where every vote carries the same weight and is equal at the UN General Assembly, so small countries matter very much. While the European countries, China, Russia, and the US are mighty, the support of small countries make a difference when it comes to supporting resolutions that come before the general assembly. Part of this support comes from the example we set for small nations: if we can stand up for ourselves, so can they. This also builds bridges and creates allies.

Small Victories Make Big Impacts

One day, as I grabbed lunch at the UN cafeteria with my advisor, I noticed that while there was halal food for Muslims, there was no kosher food at the cafeteria. Why, I asked my advisor. "Because it's just you," came the answer, implying I was the only one who cared about kosher food in the building. This made no sense, and it's also untrue. I told him on the spot, let's change it. I asked to have a meeting with the person who was in charge of the management at the UN. This turned out to be the Undersecretary for Management, Yukio Takasu, who was from Japan.

Before the meeting, we had to explain what it was about. In polite but strong terms, I wrote to the undersecretary that we wanted to have kosher food at the UN cafeterias, just as it offered special food for other religions and dietary restrictions and requirements. He was very nervous, because he thought it meant setting up a special kosher kitchen to prepare the food. At the start of the meeting, I told him to relax. There was no need to build a new kitchen. There was a much easier solution: there are many Jewish caterers in New York. I gave him the names of several companies that would deliver kosher food. He loved the idea. Two weeks after the meeting, he called to say that kosher food would be in the cafeteria the next day.

I was a bit worried that no one would buy the food, and that I had made such a fuss over something that seemed trivial. Every week we have a staff meeting in our mission, which is outside the UN building. I decided to relocate the meeting to the UN this time and asked the team to buy lunch from the kosher area so that I could at least guarantee some sales on the first day. I had no reason to worry; when we gathered to buy lunch after the meeting, everything was sold out! People feel that kosher food is healthy, so it is popular. Why is this so important? It sends a message in a peaceful and I dare say, an enjoyable way: Israel is part of the UN. We have respect for others but we demand to be respected as well, including respect for our foods, traditions, and customs.

We also held many events around the Jewish holidays at the UN, also a first. While many ambassadors live in New York and know about Jewish holidays, they don't understand what they really mean. I showed them by hosting them together with my wife, Talie, and my children, Aviad, Hila, and Shira, for celebrations of Passover, Hanukkah, and others. For the first time, many ambassadors became familiar with Israel's history and traditions. For example, we had a mock Passover Seder at the UN. I was unsure who would attend, but happily about seventy-five ambassadors joined us. I hosted this event for four consecutive years, and many ambassadors came back, including the ambassador from Turkey, who attended twice. It helped foster a better working relationship between us, even though we were on opposite sides of the negotiating table.

I led a complicated process that resulted in the UN designating Yom Kippur as an official holiday, so that no official meetings are held on that day, and employees can choose to come to work or not. I joke that now the UN has a day to repent for all the resolutions they helped pass against Israel.

These small steps contributed to a larger issue, which is the mainstreaming of anti-Zionism or the wholesale rejection not just of Israeli policy points, but of the idea of a Jewish state and its right to exist. This form of anti-Zionism is becoming a respectable position among people and nations who would otherwise not support the elimination of a country. Obviously allowing these ideas to fester and grow has an adverse effect on Israeli security.

Many people mistakenly blame Israel for the violence and unrest at its borders and with Palestinian terror groups. The claim is essentially that we are "occupying" the Palestinian "territories" of the Palestinian people. We are not the ones subjugating a people; the Palestinian leadership has shown itself to be quite effective at holding back its own people from prosperity and freedom. In fact, Israel's enemies are dedicated to destroying us long before we set foot on Gaza or Judea and Samaria. We've also voluntarily handed over more land taken in war than any nation in the world.

Many moderate Arab countries, both their people and representatives, understand what we understood years ago: it's not because of us that we don't resolve the conflict. It's because of the Palestinians. They are tired of it too. They say to the Palestinians, "Enough. Sit down. Negotiate with the Israelis. If you are not willing to do it, we are going to do it."

Not long after the devastating Passover attack in the Chabad synagogue outside San Diego in Poway, California on April 27, 2019, we brought the synagogue's rabbi, who was also injured in the attack, Rabbi Yisroel Goldstein, to speak at the general assembly. It was a special session of the UN General Assembly, which I initiated around the issue of fighting antisemitism. It was both moving and inspiring to hear the rabbi address world leaders and share with them the events of that day, which did not change the rabbi's commitment and belief. On the contrary, it made them stronger.

During one of the debates about Israel in the security council, I decided to focus on the eternal rights of the Jewish people to the land of Israel by quoting the Bible. I put the yarmulke on my head to deliver the speech. Some ambassadors were shocked at my direct approach, but the speech went viral. It eventually came to be known as the Biblical Speech in the UN Security Council. For some professional diplomats, to hear and see a colleague use the

Bible was awkward and uncomfortable. It was important, because it made clear our biblical rights to the land. Diplomacy is fine, but to be effective in establishing a position, you have to go outside the confines of protocol. One has to bring one's inner values and emotions to the table.

Professional diplomats do not like to create situations where emotions may be on display. For the first time, I brought this biblical claim to the table, and it brought my claims respect. It only added to the rights we have according to international law. Sometimes the professional staff I worked with from the foreign service didn't always feel comfortable when they learned about my creative methods. Only after they saw the impact of these events did they realize that there is no one textbook for effective diplomacy. I encouraged them to bring their own personal stories and emotions to the fore. They learned from me how to create an interest in what we were saying. Once you capture your colleagues' attention, you can deliver the message effectively.

Such outspoken events allowed me to open the doors and win the hearts and minds of those who might have been reluctant to show any affinity toward Israel, and start a dialogue. Before I brought Israel to the UN, most only knew one side of the story, which was the anti-Israel side. I got the attention of people who previously had not given Israel much thought. It absolutely changed the landscape. Bringing ambassadors from major countries to Israel changed our position in the world and strengthened our security. It changed voting patterns in the UN. One example is Mexico. I was able to build a relationship with the country through its ambassador. He came to Israel to visit, and afterward, he started to pay attention to any resolution that was connected with Israel. He was able to have a dialogue with his superiors in Mexico City about Israel. As a result, we saw progress in Mexico's voting pattern on resolutions. Mexico is a big country with strong alliances, so it was no small accomplishment to convince them to learn about and consider our side of issues.

CHAPTER FOUR

Open Doors = Open Minds

Relationships matter.

Diplomacy is an active pursuit that has ebbs and flows. Those engaged in it must understand that to be productive, one should not expect to win all the time, nor should they try to appease everybody all the time, smooth the way for adversaries, or placate hostile actors. Rather, diplomacy should be an integral part of a nation's policy to advance its interests, stability, and international influence. These goals are helped by reaching out to those who understand your concerns, are sympathetic to your goals, and with whom you have shared values and aspirations. The importance of genuine friendships should never be underestimated, not only in their value to policymaking, but because they enable deeper understanding, empathy, and compassion between nations and people. Friends understand each other. Enemies don't. In short, while nations must be sovereign, they also need friends. As in everyday life, diplomacy can test true friendships during times of crises, when we are under fire or under diplomatic attack. Those are the times when we see who our real friends are and who is willing to pay a price while standing with us.

Even in what is generally thought of as a bastion of hostility toward Israel, the UN is a place where many friends can and should be made. I made it my business to do so. For me, the job was not one of formality and socializing. It was a real and important opportunity to make headway in the advancement of Israeli interests, which frankly, are also in the best interests of regional and international peace and global prosperity. The UN made it possible for me to build relationships with representatives from countries I would not have open access to in any other way.

Think of this: any time a special envoy from Israel travels to an Arab country, it has to be done with the utmost discretion. If such visits were to be discussed publicly, they could become an issue that could result in political backlash or even violence from extremists and terrorists. At the UN in New York, you can meet anyone, any time, in a legitimate and open forum free from the anxiety of those who are determined to see you fail. Indeed, such exchanges between adversaries and friends are expected, which is why the UN is a useful tool despite criticisms about its effectiveness in the twenty-first century. The development of strong personal relationships there, or anywhere (on or off the playing field), are helpful in an assortment of endeavors, including creating a wide variety of allies, trade deals, and peace negotiations.

All countries rely on allies, including at the UN. One result of this is that many countries, especially those in similar geographic areas, or that have other commonalities whether ideologically, culturally, or economically, form strategic alliances. Even though there is an underlying competition between nations at the UN, being a member of such a group gives you opportunities to accomplish goals as a united front. Many UN-elected positions are allocated to regional groups. As a result, I often found myself working or negotiating with several countries at once in many instances, trying to build support within a regional group for our positions.

A UN group can have significant influence when decisions are made in the capitals of the countries they represent. Unfortunately, some of these groups also create a dynamic that is openly hostile to Israel, such as the Group of 77[24] or G-77, nonaligned countries who were not willing to take sides during the Cold War, for or against the US or the Soviet Union. The G-77 was established on June 15, 1964 by seventy-seven developing countries. Today, the membership has increased to 134 countries, so the original name honors its historical significance. It's the largest intergovernmental organization of developing countries at the UN and provides a means for members to express and promote their collective economic interests and enhance their joint negotiating capacity on all major international economic issues within the UN. However, there is pressure from some members of the group to conform when voting on anti-Israel resolutions. This meant I had to work with individual ambassadors away from the pressure of the group, and this was much more productive in terms of changing the way many member states viewed Israel.

Making personal, one-on-one connections with individual ambassadors in the G-77 enabled me to show the human side of my country, something often lacking in discussions about Israel inside the UN. These men and women would no longer be afraid to speak on our behalf publicly, which was important and helped change others' attitudes toward Israel. In particular, there's my friendship with the ambassadors from Singapore and India, both countries that are strong and active members of the G-77. In a few situations, both were willing to lead efforts on our behalf publicly in order to steer the G-77 toward our direction.

For many nations, the UN ambassador is also the person who reflects the world back to their home country, which includes global trends, challenges, and opportunities. In many countries, the UN ambassador is a key figure in the inner circle of the head of state. That's why it is so important to build relationships at the UN—it can and does make a difference because, in many cases, it is your direct pipeline to a country's leader. Many of these ambassadors have cabinet positions in their governments. Even in the US, depending on the administration in power, when it comes to foreign policy, the UN ambassador is a crucial element in the decision-making process. While some kinds of ambassadorships may seem purely ceremonial, a UN ambassadorship is not. Once a term at the UN is over, you can be assured that many ambassadors turn their attention to political positions in their home countries, some going on to become heads of state or ministers of foreign affairs. It is useful to have existing relationships with such people.

Any time I saw an opportunity to meet someone, I was often the initiator and reached out to them first. Honestly, there were ambassadors who did not want to approach me, such was the hostility toward my country at the UN. It was up to me to make the first move, and I was happy to do so. I tried to never miss an opportunity and never judged a person by the size of the country they represented or its economic or military power or prowess. I didn't even make judgments based on their behavior toward anti-Israeli resolutions at the UN. If I think I can change a mind, I am going to make the effort. That's what foreign policy should engage itself with.

If making friends with and getting to know people and their families outside of my normal social and professional circle was eye-opening for me, and broadened my view, it was true for the other person as well. When people get to know you, and the history of a place or an event you're representing, familiarity does not breed contempt; rather, it is the best way to achieve understanding and a working relationship. It lays the foundation for allies when pursuing stability and national security.

I made sure that the Israeli UN mission was accessible to other nations' representatives during both the Obama administration, when Samantha Power served as the US representative, and the Trump administration, when Nikki Haley came on board. Many would come to me and ask if I could speak with the US or Russia on their behalf or arrange a meeting. If I could do it, I would. For instance, the president of a small, friendly country from Eastern Europe wanted to come to Washington to have a meeting with then-president Donald Trump. The ministry of foreign affairs of that country could not get a confirmation of a meeting. Oftentimes, the protocol is for smaller countries to meet with the secretary of state instead of the president. The country asked me to help them get the meeting, and that is what I did. Similar instances and requests also happened during the Obama administration.

It was a way for me to help and show my sincerity. Sometimes there was a bilateral issue or problem with one country, and I was able to speak not only with the US mission, but also with US congressmen and senators who would take my call because I had a personal relationship with them. I was always happy to facilitate introductions or appeals for other ambassadors whenever I could. The long-lasting benefits of being generous builds strong alliances and helps to gain the respect of friend and foe alike.

Reaching Across Aisles

I was never afraid to extend a hand to people who on the face of it would not be natural or "important" allies, and I did it many times. For instance, I often found myself arguing with the Turkish ambassador on a variety of issues, mainly concerning the conflict with the Palestinians. We have a complicated relationship with Turkey. At one point, Ambassador Haley and I were leading a resolution to condemn Hamas, and the Turkish ambassador had received direct instructions from President Recep Tayyip Erdoğan to fight it. Turkey is a NATO member, but it allows Hamas to operate from its territory. Senior Hamas officials are living and working on Turkish soil with the blessing of the Turkish authorities. Hamas is an off-shoot of the Muslim Brotherhood, a terror group. If the UN would condemn Hamas, it would embarrass the leader of Turkey.

Erdoğan is a difficult man to trust. He is known for making radical statements that contain incitement against Israel[25] and using the Palestinian conflict for his domestic political purposes. He had already used the sensitive situation in Jerusalem to provoke violence. He used the situation in Gaza to enhance his image in the Arab world. It's a rollercoaster ride with Turkey, so we must always proceed with caution when dealing with that country.

I kept this in mind when dealing with the Turkish ambassador. At one point, we were at loggerheads with the Turkish ambassador on an anti-Israeli issue. Despite that, we were able to meet and have a meaningful dialogue. Our relationship survived. I hosted the ambassador in my family's home in New York. While that visit didn't sit comfortably with some people in both Turkey and Israel, it helped further discussion and bridge-building. I learned many things that were going on behind closed doors. I was able to get more support for certain resolutions from Turkey and others than I would have, had I not made the effort to extend a hand.

Openness to dialogue with everyone who is willing has meaning and can be productive. Although Erdoğan must be watched carefully, following many years of contentious relations, in December 2020, he said publicly that "Turkey wants to improve its relations with Israel. Our intelligence cooperation with Israel is ongoing." The country also altered its foreign policy toward the entire Middle East region and Israel in particular. Three weeks earlier, in November 2020, former Admiral Cihat Yaycı, a close associate of Erdoğan, proposed a shared maritime border deal with Israel. I attribute this in great part to the policies and strategies I describe here. He had also predictably backtracked on this sentiment, claiming later that Gaza had "no right in humanity"[26] and that Jerusalem belongs to Turkey.[27]

In April 2021, there were several reports that Turkey wanted to resend an ambassador to Tel Aviv once the Israeli government committed to simultaneously reciprocating the measure.[28] However, our main point of contention remains: Hamas uses Turkey as a base of operations. As a result, Israel did not move forward with this proposal.[29] Still, there is hope. At one time, Turkey was a vital economic, diplomatic, and defense partner for Israel. That is unfortunately less so today. It is also important to note that

Turkey and Israel have never severed diplomatic ties, despite our issues with Hamas's presence in that country over the years.

In April 2021, Dr. Hakan Yurdakul, a board member of the Turkish President's Committee for Economic Policies, attended a European Jewish Parliament conference focused on a positive and restorative agenda between the two nations. Turkey also wants to normalize relations with other countries in the region—it sees the writing on the wall, that placating terrorists and hosting Hamas is not the way to move forward in the modern world. As a result, it has reached out to Cairo. In March 2021, Turkish authorities ordered Istanbul-based news channels affiliated with the Muslim Brotherhood to stop airing criticism of Egypt.[30] This is a signal that the Erdoğan government could begin to remove or stifle senior Hamas leaders living and working out of Istanbul. Let us wait and see.

In March 2021, Prime Minister Netanyahu, while speaking at a Likud campaign event in Bat Yam, confirmed to the world that Israel was engaged in talks with Turkey about natural gas production in the eastern Mediterranean Sea. Dialogue is always possible and welcome. The prime minister said that the recent ongoing talks with Turkey were productive, and that similarly fruitful discussions were taking place with Egypt, Greece, and Cyprus, all focused on the exportation of this gas to Europe.

However, we have consistently managed to successfully separate economics and politics when it comes to humanitarian issues. As more countries work with Israel and normalize diplomatic relations, which has accelerated since 2015, Turkey sees its growing isolation. Moreover, Turkey's strained relations with the US is worrisome. It's a difficult situation but one that we are willing to continue to work on. We remain suspicious and cautious.

Like other countries in the region, Turkey is also fearful of nuclear developments in Iran, along with the growing influence the country has over certain factions in the region. Turkey is right to want to curb this, and it can do so by working with Israel in a more normalized and focused fashion. It is unstable—one day, we have common interests, and the next day, Erdoğan incites against Israel. Very carefully, we continue to come to the table whenever possible with honesty but also with great caution.

Working relationships at the UN and otherwise are beneficial for Israeli security in ways beyond restorative cross-border politics. A Muslim ambassador from another important but small country met with me discreetly several times over the years, and a friendship emerged. We hosted him and his family, and he reciprocated. When the time came to promote a resolution condemning the US embassy move to Jerusalem, he had no choice but to support it, as the repercussions for him at home and with other colleagues would have been great if he hadn't. However, he did share information about the resolution with me beforehand, and I was able to amend its inflammatory language. He did it in a smart way; he didn't work against his instructions, but sharing the information with me privately allowed me to prepare myself, alert our allies, and get them involved in our successful efforts to change the resolution's wording.

On other occasions, I would meet with Muslim ambassadors in private homes. The close relationship with one Muslim country that we enjoy today started at the UN, when I met its ambassador at the apartment of a Jewish American leader. This way, the Muslim ambassador could say with honesty that he was going to a cocktail party—an event he did not need his home officer's permission to attend. This intimate social event, where we expressed our individual humanity in a comfortable setting, led to meaningful cooperation later on.

In 2016, I visited the United Arab Emirates (UAE) and saw the Arabian (Persian) Gulf and the country of Iran with my own eyes. This was not an easy trip to arrange, and it had to be done with great discretion. Until 2020, Israelis were banned from visiting the UAE. I was attending a UN conference, and it was difficult to even obtain an invitation to the event. For authorities in the UAE to finally issue the invitation was a big deal. For security reasons, I could not fly on just any commercial airline, there were restrictions on which companies I could use. My security detail had to check the routes of my flights very carefully to ensure my plane would not pass over Iran (in case of an emergency we would not be forced to land there). A special visa had to be issued since the UAE did not officially recognize Israel at the time. Even at JFK airport in New York, we had problems obtaining boarding passes because airline computers would not allow Israeli passport holders to check into a flight going to the UAE. It took a while to solve that problem.

I was able to arrange a discussion with a senior official from the UAE while there. He told me that the first missile launched by Iran would likely be aimed at Abu Dhabi (the capital of the UAE), and not Jerusalem. That interaction led us to cooperate on policy fighting terrorism in the region and taking steps against Iran in the UN. As a result of this meeting and many others that focused on the aggression coming from Iran, Israel continues to work with the UAE and other countries in the region.

Today, we are on a different level of cooperation entirely than we were five or ten years ago. There are more than sixteen weekly direct flights between Tel Aviv and the UAE. During my visit in 2016, my hosts were very polite, but they made sure that I was not visible to any media outlets, and they asked me not to post any information about the trip on social media. On some occasions, they tried to avoid group photographs that included my face. Today, it is very different. When I was invited by the government of the UAE to the Dubai Expo 2020, I was shocked to see the number of media outlets that were invited to cover the event where I spoke. Many attendees wanted to take "selfies" with the visitor from Israel.

Even before signing the peace agreement, we had working relations with the UAE. All of the cooperation in New York had to be done behind closed doors. In order to have meetings, we had to coordinate a hotel room in the middle of the day, since meeting in a public area would have been too risky. I felt as if I was cheating on my wife. Before one of these meetings, I received a call from the UAE ambassador asking me to stay in the car while she sent me a new location for the meeting. Apparently, the hotel we were scheduled to meet at was also hosting celebrity Kim Kardashian, who attracted a lot of media that we wanted to avoid.

Ambassador Nikki Haley brought a new momentum to the role of ambassador to the US, and her collaborative spirit throws into high relief how good working relationships matter in getting things done. She had no problem expressing open and public support for Israel. I had heard about Nikki when she became the first US governor to pass an anti-BDS (Boycott, Divestment, and Sanctions movement) legislation.[31] I asked my staff to coordinate a visit to South Carolina at the beginning of my UN appointment, but because of a series of events at the UN, it had to be canceled.

It was a great surprise to hear she was coming to the UN. When a new ambassador arrives, it is customary to greet the most important countries first. After she called on the ambassadors from France and England, she "ditched" protocol and called on me.[32] I could not have been more flattered. Nikki assured me it would be a different era when she came into the office. Like me, she came to the position after a long political career. Both of us were criticized for our lack of experience in foreign affairs and diplomacy and for our political backgrounds. I told her from my personal experience the best thing to do is ignore such criticisms, but instead, to go with your truth.

We developed a personal relationship, my family and hers, which proved to be important in terms of working together as allies. We had moments of losses and victories. I was also happy to host her first of many visits to Israel. Over our years of working together, I came to appreciate her character, thoughtfulness, and intelligence.

My wife, Talie, and I were lucky to spend time with Nikki and her husband, Michael, and we enjoy an ongoing friendship today. We had an understanding as friends that any event I held in my apartment would include an invitation to the Haley's, and Nikki reciprocated in the same way. They joined us at our Hanukkah party; likewise, my wife and I attended Christmas parties and many dinners with fascinating guests like Henry Kissinger, and Ivanka and Jared Kushner. Oftentimes I would meet ambassadors with whom we had no diplomatic relations. It was a good way to break the ice and begin to create personal bonds that could have far-reaching implications in policymaking. I had the pleasure of getting to know her unique and talented son, Nalin, who came to intern at the Israeli mission.

Nikki had the character and courage to say the truth, and to act accordingly even when she was in a minority at the UN. When we arrived in Israel, she was welcomed everywhere with love. I remember one moment when a group of ultra-Orthodox girls were nearby while we were boarding a helicopter at the Knesset helipad. They recognized her and spontaneously ran toward her to hug her. It was a beautiful, unrehearsed moment, unplanned, authentic, and organic. These kinds of natural experiences stay with people and increase their understanding of complex issues, and underline the importance of meaningful cross-cultural friendships.

Israelis were grateful that Nikki had a chance to see the nation in a very personal way. We flew over Jerusalem and saw the ancient city from above. We flew to the south of Israel, where I showed her the borders between Israel and Jordan and Israel and Egypt. I will never forget the moment she told me to stop showing her the borders. "I can see them," she said, "where it is green, it is Israel." She understood firsthand that the idea of turning the desert green is not just a metaphor, it is a reality. We visited the communities on the border with Gaza, where she met with and spoke to the people who were appreciative of her solidarity with their challenges.

When you stand on the border and see with your own eyes the Hamas terrorists' tunnel, it makes an impact. When a mother of small children tells you about the shooting she hears outside her window during the night, that is something you remember. She was very moved by this as a mother; she identified with them. She embraced them. When Nikki went back to the UN, she could talk from firsthand experience about what she saw, and she was not shy to call out the challenges she saw for herself.

Working relationships deepen, and insights into challenges associated with your cause deepen, through shared experiences. On that trip, I took Nikki to an observation point on the border with Lebanon. We had a special briefing with a senior commander from the IDF northern command. We used electronic binoculars, high-tech devices with long-range visibility, to clearly see the activities of Hezbollah on the other side of the border. This was a clear violation of UN SC Resolution 1701, which allows only the Lebanese army to be in the region, and not Hezbollah. Yet Hezbollah builds bases near the border, takes over most of the land next to our border, and calls them "green areas" or natural preserves to prevent the UNIFIL (United Nations Interim Force in Lebanon) troops from inspecting their activities.

I told Nikki quietly that suddenly and conveniently members of the terror group have become environmentalists under the Green Without Borders movement. Our intelligence proved otherwise: that these are Hezbollah military bases. UN peacekeepers are supposed to monitor them, but they are told they cannot set foot on these areas because they are "preserves." As a result, the UN peacekeepers essentially allowed Hezbollah to acquire rockets and missiles on the border with Israel. Instead of monitoring it, they pushed off their obligation. Nikki could see this with her own eyes.

General Michael Beary, an Irish Army Major General, and at the time, the UNIFIL Head of Mission and Force Commander, was there for the meeting. He had arrived early, so General Beary was there when the IDF presented the worrying reality on the other side of the fence. Despite what he heard from the IDF, he clung to the idea that the situation was peaceful. Nikki pressed him on it and asked him how he could say that conditions were calm when she could see for herself that they weren't. It was clear that the Lebanese army was collaborating with Hezbollah. Nikki asked me when the yearly renewal of the mandate of UNIFIL in the security council would take place. I said it would be in a few weeks. She told me that we would have to improve the language of the resolution as soon as we get back to New York.

UN peacekeepers are an important force in the region, but they are often afraid to engage with Hezbollah because of the threat of violence against UNIFIL troops. In the past, when they tried to be more effective, there were attacks on UNIFIL troops, and a few Spanish soldiers died. Hezbollah was sending a message that said in effect, if you do your job, you will pay a price.

This is the dilemma of every UNIFIL commander. On the one hand, you want to protect your soldiers, but on the other hand, to fulfill your mission, you have to engage with Hezbollah, stop their activities, or at least report on them. I had no expectations that the UNIFIL troops would actually fight Hezbollah, but at the very least, I wanted them to report honestly and accurately on Hezbollah's activity. Every time UNIFIL tries to enter a suspicious site, they are blocked from doing so.

A monthly list of all the locations that barred entry would show the UN Security Council that if someone blocked peace-keepers from entering the site, there was something happening there that shouldn't be. Together with the US team, we demanded an amendment to the procedures, specifically to require periodic reports about those sites. France and Italy were not supportive of this idea; they were not open to any changes. Italy is always concerned about the wellbeing of its soldiers in the region. However, because of the special relationship with Ambassador Haley and the US team, we were able to get the attention and support of the US Mission in getting the report changed. The resolution was amended, and our demand that the UNIFIL report reflect the disturbance we witnessed was met.

Everyone Counts

It is not just Muslim countries and the US that Israel concerns itself with. Stability and strength come from opening doors across the globe. I worked strategically with different continents and groups at the UN, where group affiliation has meaning and importance. Over the years, we have found that Eastern European countries have much in common with Israel, and they are quite friendly to us. Unlike some Western European countries, Eastern Europe doesn't have a history with the Arab world. They played no part in the struggles and conflicts so familiar to France or England, for example. They were under the rule of Soviet regimes. These young countries had no political baggage tied to the Middle East and were able to form their own independent policies. Their Muslim populations in these countries are also small or nonexistent, and they experienced no wave of Muslim immigration. During such migrations, Muslims would pass through Eastern Europe to wealthier countries with larger social welfare systems and a more welcoming pretense, like Germany and Scandinavia.

It was important for me to reach out to the Eastern European countries and develop a friendship with its ambassadors. I invited the ambassadors to my home in New York and made sure they were welcome at any events we hosted at the UN. Likewise, I made it a point to accept all invitations and attend events they initiated. I noticed that the Bulgarian ambassador would attend most events I held at the UN. Bulgaria is a strong ally to Israel, so I was happy to make a connection with him. He made it a point to stand with us at every opportunity, and we did the same with them. Likewise, the ambassadors from the Czech Republic and Hungary were also loyal participants at Israeli-hosted events.

I was instrumental in making introductions for these ambassadors to any interesting sectors of the Jewish communities in New York in various important fields of science, technology, and other areas that would be helpful to their countries' economic growth. When I planned a dinner at my house, I made sure to invite influential leaders from these disciplines, so that the Eastern European ambassadors would have access to them in a relaxed and friendly atmosphere. It was gratifying to know that I had facilitated mutually beneficial relationships that helped cement new friendships between nations.

As the Czech Republic, Hungary, and Bulgaria grow more confident and economically strong, one of the ways they have and will continue to show their independence and sovereignty is the approach they have taken toward Israel. We have a great opportunity to continue to strengthen our bond with the people and governments; as young countries striving to grow, they understand and relate to Israel's challenges. I believe they will continue to reject Western Europe's automatic pro-Palestinian and anti-Israeli sentiment.

This has rattled some in the EU, as strong nations like France have grown accustomed to making decisions that were accepted readily by all EU nations. This is important because any resolution in the EU requires full consensus to pass. What has happened recently in a few cases, is that new Eastern European member nations prevented consensus. Specifically, it happened when the US embassy was moved to Jerusalem. Eastern European member nations blocked the EU's efforts to condemn the US and Israel for this legitimate and long-awaited (and promised) action.

Eastern European countries have proven to be especially great friends and allies. EU countries have a weekly meeting at the UN where anti-Israel topics, among others, are discussed. For instance, Ireland often leads the European case against Israel. As discussed, I was pushing for a resolution to condemn Hamas along with Nikki Haley in the general assembly. We had gotten a great deal of support from various members. The ambassador from Ireland, Geraldine Byrne Nason, was active in trying to sabotage our efforts by introducing another resolution condemning Israel and looking for procedural technicalities that would stop our resolution from coming to the floor. It was shameful to see this, and worse yet, no Western European country would speak on our behalf. I would, however, receive text messages about these discussions from an Eastern European member in attendance. I would give that member our perspective in a relied text, and that would be shared by one of the Eastern European ambassadors.

I spent a lot of time on the Iranian issue, because wherever you see instability in the Middle East, you can see the fingerprints of the Iranian regime. Whether it's Hezbollah in Lebanon or their proxies in Syria, Hamas in Gaza, Yemen—you name it, Iran spends billions of dollars a year promoting terrorism. The challenge to fighting Iranian influence is in Western European countries. Working with them is an ongoing process. Our friendships with Australia, Canada, and of course the US, help balance the hostility that comes from some of the Western European EU member countries. And we do share critical information and intelligence with EU countries. They can't ignore the hostilities of the Iranian regime, and as a result we are starting to see change. For example, Germany has outlawed Hezbollah, labeling them as a terror organization. We hope to see many more countries push back against Iranian aggression.

Many African countries have reaffirmed their support of Israel, but not without some effort on our part. Israel's ties with Sub-Saharan African countries date back to the mid-1950s. Diplomatic relations with most countries south of the Sahara were established after we formalized relations with Ghana. By the early 1970s, Israel had full diplomatic relations with thirty-three countries in the region. These ties were a natural expression of African affinity with Israel. Our still young nation was eager to share our experiences and expertise with newly independent African states.

As a result, we formed several mutually beneficial joint ventures, and throughout the 1950s and 1960s, Israel helped establish agricultural cooperatives, youth training programs, medical infrastructure, and industrial enterprises in Ghana, Sierra Leone, Ivory Coast, Nigeria, and other sub-Saharan countries.

After the Yom Kippur War in 1973 and the global oil crisis that followed, things changed for us in Africa. Most Sub-Saharan countries severed diplomatic ties with Israel because of the demand for compliance with the OAU (Organization of African Unity) resolution, which was sponsored by Egypt, which also called for severing relations with Israel. Only three African nations, Malawi, Lesotho, and Swaziland, maintained full diplomatic relations with Israel during this time. Some commercial ties continued, African students still participated in training courses in Israel, and Israeli science and technology and other experts remained on the continent in less official but helpful capacities.

Starting in the 1980s, diplomatic relations with Sub-Saharan countries were gradually renewed, and have recently gained momentum, as peace negotiations between Israel and many of its Arab neighbors have progressed. By the late 1990s, we had reestablished official ties with forty countries south of the Sahara.

In April 2019, Israel opened its embassy in Rwanda, fifty years after the two countries established diplomatic relations. This was eight years after opening an embassy in Ghana in 2011, which we have had diplomatic relations with since 1956. It marked the eleventh embassy we have opened on the African continent.

Rwanda President Paul Kagame has a strong relationship with Israel. This relationship has been a wonderful role model, because it shows major African countries what was possible by aligning with Israel, and that you can be aligned with Israel and still be an important player on the international stage. Seeing Rwanda work with Israel made other African countries see that the threats coming from our adversaries were not real.

Africa presents great potential for cooperation and mutual benefit. The continent has many natural resources, and we have the know-how and technology to help them exploit these resources for their peoples' benefit. One of the things I did at the UN was to bring Israeli scientists and technology experts in for one-hour information breakfasts, always making sure African ambassadors were invited. It amazed me to see these men and women stay until the end. They were fascinated with the solutions we offered, especially around water processing, quality control, and delivery.

Another geopolitical group we've made headway with is the Asia Pacific, a region consisting of the whole of Asia as well as the countries of the Pacific Rim. Many of these countries are part of the G-77 I talked about earlier. As the G-77 became larger and welcomed more Asian country members, they too refrained from taking political sides. They tended to stay neutral when it came to Israel, but at the UN, if you stay neutral, you are against Israel. Moreover, some of these Asian Pacific nations are Muslim, like Indonesia, so the pressure to conform against Israel can be powerful.

Nonetheless, I made a very successful visit to Singapore while at the UN. We have had diplomatic relations with the country since 1969, and they are a friendly nation to Israel. Everybody in Singapore still remembers that Israel was willing to lend a hand and help them build and train their army at a time when no other countries were willing to engage with them when they were forced to establish their independence in 1965.[33] Every official in the government I met started the conversation by thanking me for Israel's support. I made a mental note that Israel's leaders in the 1960s were smart to invest in building those strong bonds we enjoy today.

We focused on technological cooperation during my meeting with the Singapore minister of foreign affairs, and I asked him to check on the possibility of helping us strengthen ties with Indonesia. Unfortunately, the answer I received was that while they would like to have stronger relations with Israel, the "timing" was not right because elections were coming up in the country. Many of its politicians use the issue of the Palestinians and holy sites in Jerusalem to mobilize votes. It was disappointing but not surprising. Many Muslim countries use the same strategies to win votes; doing so is a typical tool for domestic politics in these places. Indonesia has the largest Muslim population in the world, and it is unfortunate that it allows radical ideas to block the great potential it would offer the country through cooperation with Israel.

In March 2016, Prime Minister Netanyahu again called for normalization of ties with Indonesia, citing the many opportunities we have for bilateral cooperation. However, Indonesia refused, saying it will only consider normalization when Palestinians achieve independence. In 2018, Yahya Cholil Staquf, a member of the Presidential Advisory Council, visited Israel to meet the prime minister, and joined a Jewish Forum. The Indonesian public viewed the visit negatively—some statistics say the majority of Indonesians view Israel negatively. The ongoing incitement will make it harder in the future, but as we can see, the radical Muslim groups pose a threat to Indonesia's stability regardless of their approach to Israel. I know that Indonesian culture values education, and there is so much we can share with them. I believe our relationship will be cemented in time. However, we have been able to create ties on some economic issues, and I believe that the future will open new opportunities to both countries.

The Pacific Islands are a mighty phenomenon. These small islands, some with only a few thousand citizens each, are great friends of Israel. They are Christians who know the Bible and love the Holy Land. I admire them greatly. Whenever they requested my support in terms of securing funding from the US, again, I was happy to facilitate however I could. They always stand with Israel at the UN, and on this issue they are unwilling to compromise. One of the Pacific Island ambassadors once told me that Iran had tried to buy their support, but he said no matter what they offer, he will never vote against Israel, because it would be like voting against himself.

Israel creates a lot of emotion in people, and I never take that for granted. Likewise, I would never take the tiny Pacific Islands for granted. I would invite the ambassadors for regular meetings to see how we could help them, and it was fascinating to learn about the issues that were important to them. For example, I learned that they have a problem with diabetes and obesity, so we put them in touch with Israeli nutrition and medical experts. I also invited them to visit Israel, and the trip was very successful. To see their faith come alive at the holy sites was truly remarkable; it was the highlight of their visit—for them and for me.

The ambassador of Palau, Dr. Caleb Otto, became a good friend of mine. He was so devoted to us that he made sure to attend every debate where Israel was discussed. The Palau mission was tiny, with maybe two or three staff members, but I used to joke with my own staff that even during Jewish holidays, when we could not participate in the debates, we were always represented because I trusted that my dear friend Caleb would be there. Unfortunately, after a trip to Israel, he went home to Palau and passed away in 2018. What a lovely man. I wrote a sincere letter to his family and shared treasured memories of our friendship when he passed, and I miss him to this day.

Small countries are absolutely worth the effort. However, not all small countries are easy to connect with. The Caribbean can be difficult. Unlike the Pacific Islands, the Caribbean countries are often aligned with Latin American groups at the UN. Some of these groups in the past had a socialist agenda and were tied to the Arab League. A willingness to engage in any way we can brings some hope. There was a diplomat in our office who was in charge of relations between Israel and the Caribbean islands. He often flew back and forth, and whenever I saw him I'd joke that he had the best position in representing Israel to islands many people think of as paradise. I often talked to him about how we could help the Caribbean islands, and he informed me that some of the islands had a problem with crime. We put them in touch with our experts in the field of crime prevention. He asked me to host a lunch for the UN ambassadors of the Caribbean Islands, and during that lunch, I learned about the need for many of these islands to have technology that helps combat crime, technology Israel can provide.

There are other positive signs: Brazil says they want to move its embassy to Jerusalem, and I am hopeful that will happen. We set a precedent with Guatemala and Honduras, as they moved their embassies to Jerusalem. We were also able to create some change in our relationship with Costa Rica and Mexico. Today, Mexico doesn't automatically vote against us at the UN.

Unfortunately, Iran is heavily invested in South America. There is a link between terror in Latin America and Iran in the form of training camps and Jewish-targeted violence. We know, for example, that some attacks on Jewish communities in Argentina were initiated by Iran. Venezuela and Bolivia, in particular, cling to leftist ideology, and choose to identify with anti-Israel propaganda. The leadership does fine, but their people continue to suffer.

However, we saw an opening to engage in South America because of what is happening with the Venezuelan economic crisis. Everyone can look at the regimes in Venezuela and Cuba and understand that the radical leftist rhetoric creates chaos and instability. In the past, Venezuela was very involved with anti-Israel initiatives; today, they are trying to survive. We become closer to countries in Central America by showing them how we can improve life in the region. We hope to see a change also in Venezuela. We hope that people in places like Venezuela will be willing to fight to change a system that deprives them of many rights and access to things we take for granted, like food, fuel, and education.

The current Venezuelan president, Nicolas Maduro, is hostile to the US and Israel. However, the interim government, run by its leader, Juan Guido, is much friendlier to us, and this government does have an unofficial representative at the UN. He is not an ambassador; however, countries like the US, Israel, and some other democracies recognize him and work with him. It was important for me to meet with him, even though he was not in a position to vote on any resolutions, because he is the representative of the interim government. I made it a point to meet with the representatives every few weeks to offer advice and provide any help in making connections. I found it exciting and important to take part in the process of building a positive future for the people of Venezuela, and I believe one day they will be able to gain their freedom and prosper. When that day comes, Israel will be there for the people of Venezuela in their efforts to reconstruct their nation.

Relationship building, like diplomacy, is quiet and long term. In politics, people say negative things about you behind closed doors, while in public, they are nice. At the UN, countries admire Israel quietly, while condemning it in public. Countries are willing to engage despite this, and we prove it by the fact that of the UN's 193 member states, Israel holds formal relations with more than 160 countries, and even more informally behind closed doors. Those doors will open in time, I am sure of it. The more doors that open, the more secure Israel becomes.

I encourage the leaders of these countries to stop hiding and publicly declare their relations with Israel. Many have done so already, in their own way. For example, many of the UN diplomats who formally denounced or openly spoke out against Israel actually voted for me to head the UN legal committee, indirectly honoring me with the coveted position of being the first Israeli ambassador to lead a UN committee. This is not a small accomplishment, and it should inspire future and current diplomats, ambassadors, and others in positions of influence. Never stop extending your hand, even to those who may not want to reach back in friendship. In my experience, many surprising people are willing to take a seat with you and talk about difficult subjects. The rejection of others does not mean you should not keep trying. We can and we should continue the conversation with whomever is willing to listen.

CHAPTER FIVE

Israel Should Not Wait for Permission to Act

We must be confident about making autonomous decisions.

The security of Israel depends on its ability to make its own decisions, especially around defense and national security issues. Our robustness comes not just from military defense, but through strength created by maintaining ties and relationships with existing allies and forming new ones. However, we can't and shouldn't depend on others to give us the green light to act in defense of ourselves, to forward new ideas, or in decisions about how we face new challenges. We certainly cannot allow others to choose our friends for us. Further, standing still and waiting for permission while others are taking action is unwise and dangerous.

This point was crystalized for me as I started to build my UN connections, including with UN ambassadors from countries that we had yet to establish diplomatic ties with, and several Arab leaders. At the start of my tenure, I would report back to Jerusalem on any inroads and developments with Arab colleagues at the UN. I asked for instructions regarding the possibilities of moving forward and strengthening the relations with those colleagues. The answer I received was that I should not move forward, and wait, at least for the time being, because these were sensitive relationships that were being handled directly by some of our security agencies. These individuals claimed to have the best rapport with some of the Arab leaders in the region. Each time I saw that there was a potential opening with an ambassador or a leader of an Arab country, instead of getting affirmation or congratulations, the immediate response was not to touch it. That's when I realized there were different interests and sometimes even contradictory and certainly competing interests between different agencies. More than once, I was told, "Stay in your lane," "We have it covered," or "We don't need your help."

In the beginning of my UN tenure, I was polite to my colleagues in Jerusalem and waited for them to respond regarding those sensitive issues. After a few months of seeing no progress, I realized that reply was not forthcoming. Eventually, processes continued with or without you. I decided to be part of what was going on at the UN as an active participant instead of an observer. From my experience in public life, I knew that you can never satisfy everyone all the time. If you try to do that, you quickly become ineffectual and irrelevant. There is always someone with a different opinion, a different agency with claims that it can do things better than you.

In order to lead change at the UN, I had to be strongly committed to being tough not only with external adversaries but sometimes also with those in my own government. It's natural that you have competition even when you are ostensibly working toward the same goal. It's like a sports team; players want to be recognized for their individual achievement in winning the game. I think this is healthy, which is why it didn't deter me when someone on my own team tried to keep me out of the loop. It's all part of the game. I was at the UN to fight for my position and my ideas, and that's what I would do.

In Israel, we want to move forward with relations with as many Arab countries as we can. In one instance when I wanted to make a connection with an Arab representative, I faced resistance from every direction. The Israeli ministry of foreign affairs had made some inroads in the past with that country. The prime minister's office, through the National Security Council, was involved separately, the military intelligence had their own connections, and the Mossad was already cooperating with some agencies in this country as well. There we were, in a situation with at least four different agencies developing connections with that country. I was not sure that I should get involved, but once my colleagues at the UN asked me to meet and brought up concrete ideas for cooperation, I decided to step in to invest in the relationship and work together with that strategically important country.

I was cooperative and polite but also understood I had to do things myself and report after I had achieved something and not ask for any pre-approval. I saw similar tendencies and tensions in other missions to the UN when other countries had to deal with us on sensitive issues. In every strong democracy, you find similar competition among agencies and individuals, including the US, where I saw a structured tension between the US mission to the UN, the White House, the State Department, and other agencies. I knew such competition shouldn't hold me back from reaching out on my own in order to move forward.

My nature is to be cooperative and collaborative, but I won't let people bypass me or not include me when it comes to policy design. I was not willing to compromise on that. I was willing to give away public credit and media exposure to others in the government in exchange for a dynamic policy role. This was unusual when you come from the heat of Israeli politics, where claiming credit for accomplishments is the bread and butter of every politician. After a few months at the UN, I realized that in diplomacy it is quite the opposite. If you want to be effective, you have to keep a low profile during the process, and even after, when the mission is complete. You have to allow others to claim the fame. For someone who came from politics, it felt strange to open the newspaper and see others scoring points I had won. But I knew it was not at my expense; it served the goal I was sent to accomplish, and it allowed me to become a much stronger player in the international diplomatic arena. I was very satisfied and proud of the accomplishments themselves, even when my name or the work of the mission to the UN was omitted.

There are times when you have to step on a few toes to blaze a righteous and secure path. It's safer to participate in discussions of issues that directly concern you during the decision-making process, not after, even if that input is met with resistance. I was most productive and effective, especially with work directly related to strengthening Israel's ties with its neighbors and with global partners, when I built my own friendships and networks, and made my own decisions about UN decisions and events that directly affected Israel.

My experience is a micro example of how Israel can and should act on a macro level. Yes, we must work with a variety of partners, forge new relationships, consider the advice of those outside our circle, and take counsel from diverse sources. Ultimately, though, we must always make our own decisions. If I know I have done the right thing, I accept criticism and am comfortable with the disapproval of outsiders and even those on my side.

In using my position to lead change, I ignited a process of reaching out on my own to representatives of countries with whom Israel does not have diplomatic relations. The results speak for themselves. Forging relations with countries we had no diplomatic ties with, promoting the opening of official offices in our capital, and even moving an embassy to Jerusalem, all started in New York, in the halls of the UN.

As I've said, I come from a public service background. I served as a member of the Knesset between February 2009 until August 2015, including as deputy minister of defense, and as minister of science and technology. I did not come to the UN as a professional diplomat. Many of the rituals and traditions of diplomacy, like waiting for instructions, wording everything you say so as not to offend anyone, and remaining silent for the sake of propriety in the face of hypocrisy, didn't work for me, nor does it work for Israel. As a public servant, I was accustomed to making decisions autonomously and on the spot. In contrast, most of my fellow ambassadors would ask for directives before making nearly any decision. My colleagues would not confront anyone until they had permission to do so, and even then, there was reticence around airing disagreements, even privately, and certainly not publicly. I come from an atmosphere of debate and engagement, and that's what I brought to my role as ambassador. It may have put people off initially, but it was disarming, and I believe, quite effective in the long run.

I was also fortunate to be in a unique situation at the UN, one that afforded me the ability to meet a variety of world leaders and influencers. As I have noted, as an Israeli public official, reaching out to certain people in most other public forums, especially in the Arab world, often results in an undesirable backlash—not simply criticism, but it would cause the relationship to take a few steps backward, not forward. As a representative working at the UN, this is not the case. It is expected and encouraged that you talk with colleagues no matter what part of the world they represent. I took full advantage of this opportunity. However, I was cautious about broadcasting sensitive meetings too widely; even UN-sanctioned events or social gatherings could raise some eyebrows.

As a result, I was strategic about what I shared about these meetings publicly, something I learned from Prime Minister Netanyahu. A talented leader who believes in full control of the flow of information, he would tell you only what you needed to know at the time. In Hebrew, we call this quality *lemader*. It's a way of compartmentalizing information and limiting its exposure. When I told him about a meeting I had with a particular person from a certain country, he advised me not to write a report and keep it between us. The power of the strategic control of information was useful in my ability to become a trusted associate to many in sensitive positions, particularly when it came to dealing with the Arab world.

Never Waste the Opportunity to Influence

My role was further rarified for four out of the five years I served at the UN. Prime Minister Netanyahu did not want to appoint a foreign minister at the outset of his fourth government. Frankly, I think he wanted to be in charge and prevent anyone in the party from gaining experience that may be seen as competitive later on. As a consequence, during the first four years of my UN tenure, the prime minister served in a dual role, acting also as Israel's minister of foreign affairs. His schedule was quite full. He was dealing with numerous domestic security and economic issues, as well as an ongoing internal political crisis. None of this left him a lot of time to deal with foreign affairs, which gave me a wide berth to take action in the international arena.

This made my position much more influential in terms of policymaking, since there was not a layer between the prime minister and me when it came to foreign policy discussions. When someone wanted to meet a senior official from Israel and the prime minister was busy, or if someone wanted to send a message to Israel, I was the point person during those years. I would report directly to the prime minister about strategic meetings with international players. He and I would discuss decisions to be made on important votes at the UN and policy issues outside the scope of the UN. There were always tensions or debates when I had to get the prime minister's approval and when I took a decision myself regarding votes at the UN.

In some cases, I would make an autonomous decision because of time differences, otherwise I would have had to wake up the prime minister in the middle of the night in Israel. I used to joke with my wife that it is always a lose-lose situation. When I woke him to discuss an urgent issue, he asked me why I had bothered him with such a question. "Take the decision on those kinds of votes yourself." If I would not call him and decide on my own, he would be upset that I acted without consulting him. When the Obama administration decided at the last minute to change its vote regarding the US-Cuba embargo, Ambassador Samantha Power called me and gave me a heads-up that the US would abstain from the vote after a tradition lasting many years of voting against it.

For years, it was only the US and Israel that voted against that resolution. For me, it was important to stand with our closest ally on an issue that was important to them. I instructed my office to make sure that I would personally be present at that vote. I had to decide whether to follow the US and abstain. It was important for me to show to our American colleagues and other nations that it's a two-way relationship, and that we also know how to stand by our friends. In the past, at the end of every vote, I took a picture of the screen that showed that only the US and Israel had voted against the resolution.[34]

That year would be different. Power knew we were following the US on the issue. She did not want us to vote against it, because she was going to unexpectedly change the US voting pattern. It was a late night in New York, and everybody was sleeping in Israel. I told her that we would change our vote as well, since our goal has always been to show solidarity with the US. She stressed the importance of keeping it a secret, since the US wanted to create some drama and momentum for their policy shift toward Cuba. I told her I would send a classified telegram to Jerusalem seeking approval for my decision. I told her that if she didn't hear from me in the morning, it meant that our vote had been approved and that I would be there for it in the morning.

After the call, I rushed to my office to send the telegram to Jerusalem, knowing that by the time I woke up the next day, the approval would be there. It was a non-issue, and I did not expect any surprises. The surprise came from a different direction. When I woke up, I saw that one of the international news agencies published a report that the US would change its vote. The secret was *not* kept. It happens, but I was surprised that morning when Ambassador Power approached me in the general assembly and told me that she "was disappointed that the Israelis can't keep a secret." I was shocked, since I had not discussed the matter with anyone since our call the night before. She continued, "I know it was not you behind it, but I have connections with the news agency, and we know for sure that the leak came from Jerusalem."

After I did my homework, I discovered she was right. I was ashamed of that leak, and after that incident, I always made sure that all sensitive discussions took place over a secure line we have at our mission. When you send a telegram to more than one person, you never know where the leak is. However, when you speak directly with the prime minister, you know for sure that there are no leaks. If the information gets out, then it was his decision to release it. The more time I spent in the position, and the more experience I had, the more comfortable I was in making voting decisions on my own. If someone from the government expressed displeasure, I would simply tell them they could speak with the prime minister about it. I knew he was very busy and that he trusted my common sense. Only on the most sensitive issues would I bring him into the picture at the early stages.

After the US decided to move its embassy to Jerusalem, we were looking for other countries to follow suit. Over the years, I have cultivated important relationships with Christian evangelical leaders in the US and elsewhere, which I knew could prove important in convincing other countries with substantial evangelical populations to move their embassies. I received a phone call from an evangelical leader who suggested I talk to the president of Guatemala, Jimmy Morales, about moving that country's embassy from Tel Aviv to Jerusalem. When I checked with my colleagues back in Jerusalem, they were skeptical, once again telling me the situation was being handled and to drop it. While I listened, I didn't heed the advice. Instead, I explored the possibility through my own connections.

Israel has enjoyed a strong and decades-long friendship with Guatemala. In 1947, the Guatemalan ambassador to the UN, Dr. Jorge García Granados, cast the first vote for the creation of the state of Israel.[35] Guatemala became the first Latin American country to recognize Israel after the proclamation of the state. It is the only country outside of Israel that celebrates Israel's Independence Day, May 14. In addition, 50 percent of the population of Guatemala are evangelical Christians who love and support Israel.

Senior officials from Guatemala had approached me months earlier about a UN inquiry into the country unrelated to the embassy move, and they asked if I could facilitate help from the US administration. I was happy to do so. Based on this intervention, we further strengthened our relationship with the president and his people. They learned that I am a man of my word, and that Israel would stand with its ally.

I was eager to work with the country on moving its embassy, and I reached out to the minister of foreign affairs in Guatemala, Sandra Erica Jovel Polanco, to discuss it. I speak enough Spanish to have a conversation, but I asked one of my staff who is more fluent than I, to translate during the call to ensure we agreed on the details. It was a critical discussion with no room for misunderstanding. During that call, we went over the mechanism to make the historic decision a reality. Prime Minister Netanyahu would call President Morales and ask him to move the embassy to Jerusalem. After the phone call, the president would announce the decision and post it on social media. It was not easy for him, and many Christian evangelical leaders met with the president to give him the courage and inspiration to move forward. He agreed, and I transmitted the message to Prime Minister Netanyahu.

The next challenge was to convince the prime minister to make the call. He was skeptical. The longest-serving prime minister in Israel, who has enormous skills and experience, was afraid of embarrassment should his request not be accepted. It took some effort on my part and others to persuade him, and he did pick up the phone. We had some technical problems making the connection between the two leaders, but once both were on the line, everything went according to plan. I had no doubt this would be the case, and I guaranteed the prime minister there would be no issue. Immediately after the call, President Morales posted this message on Facebook:

> Dear people of Guatemala, today I have spoken with the Prime Minister of Israel, Benjamin Netanyahu. We talked about the excellent relationships we have had as nations since Guatemala supported the creation of the State of Israel. One of the most relevant issues was the return of the Guatemalan Embassy to Jerusalem. Therefore, I inform you that I have sent instructions to the Chancellor to initiate the respective coordination so that it is so. God bless you all.

Guatemala kept its promise; shortly after the announcement, it moved its embassy to Jerusalem.[36]

At the end of his term, former Paraguay president, Horacio Manuel Cartes Jara, announced that he would likewise move his country's embassy to Jerusalem. In my discussions with friends from Paraguay, its Jewish community, and people around the president, I talked about the timing of the move. I thought it would be best if it did not occur shortly before he left office in August 2018. We were worried that decisions taken or announced at the last minute would face claims that it was done in haste and quickly be reversed by the incoming leadership. That is exactly what happened with Paraguay. While we were happy that President Cartes made the decision, right after his election, the new president, Mario Abdo Benítez, overturned the decision.[37] Shortly after the announcement, I told the Paraguayan ambassador that we would close the Israeli embassy there, and we did.[38] I remember the conversation with the prime minister about this decision. It was an important action on our part, because it demonstrated that we viewed the reversal as a serious breach of trust, and we were not playing around. Our embassy remained closed for one year.

In the world of diplomacy, there are a few ways of responding when you want to demonstrate disappointment. You can summon the ambassador in Israel for a reprimand call. That is the least dramatic response. The second option is to recall our ambassador back to Jerusalem for consultation for a short or long period of time. The most extreme response is to close the embassy. This was the course we took, and Prime Minister Netanyahu agreed it was the right thing to do.

I sat down with the ambassador to the UN to explain to him that this was not a game, and that we were offended by the way the reversal was handled. Afterward, we closed the embassy. We strongly believe in our sovereignty over united Jerusalem. We believe all embassies should be in Jerusalem. It was a downgrade of our relationship with the country. I understand why some leaders are afraid to move their embassies to Jerusalem; the Arab League pressures them and even issues threats to cut trade and diplomatic relations. Strong leaders know that these are often empty words, or, if such ties are cut, it is temporary.

We also worked with Honduras to move its embassy to Jerusalem. I met with the president of Honduras, Juan Orlando Hernández, several times to discuss the matter. It's unusual for an ambassador to the UN to negotiate with a head of state, but we developed a warm relationship and worked out the details of a schedule of events leading up to the move. The most meaningful meeting took place in Guatemala at a ceremony for President Alejandro Eduardo Giammattei's 2019 inauguration. Many world leaders attended. President Giammattei is a friend of Israel whom I had hosted in Israel before entering his presidency, between his summer election and winter inauguration. Normally, only heads of state are invited to such occasions but in this case, he included me.

There was a long delay in the inaugural celebration. Hundreds of people were waiting for the outgoing president to show up, which took several hours. Some of the delegations left. Heads of state and senior people from the US administration were waiting for hours with nothing to do. We sat in a VIP room with Latin American heads of state and discussed different issues. President Hernandez wanted to discuss some of the issues Israelis and Hondurans shared. I told him directly in front of many leaders that for us the most important issue is the promise to move the embassy. He replied that he is onboard and he would love to discuss it privately with me after we return to the hotel. No one knew it would be hours before the inauguration got underway.

Eventually the outgoing president arrived, the ceremony started, and we went back to the hotel where we entered a small meeting room. It was very late and I was tired, but it was important for us to discuss our mutual interests with the Honduran president. The president made it clear that he was serious about his intention, but we had to do it according to his schedule. He stressed that Israel should open an economic affairs office in his country. They had opened such an office in Jerusalem and were waiting for us to open a trade office in their capital city. Afterward, they would announce the embassy move.

Because I respect him and our friendship, I promised him I will do whatever is necessary to make it happen. We opened the office in the capital, Tegucigalpa; eventually, Honduras did move its embassy to Jerusalem[39] on June 24, 2021. To mark the occasion, President Hernandez and the new Israeli prime minister, Naftali Bennett, signed several bilateral cooperation agreements at the event. Prime Minister Bennett said that the opening of the Honduran Embassy in Jerusalem, and the reopening of the Israeli

Embassy in Tegucigalpa, was "another demonstration of the deep friendship and deep connection" between the two countries.[40]

As of March 2021, Kosovo joined the US, Honduras, and Guatemala with its Jerusalem-based embassy.[41] Kosovo is the first European country and the first Muslim-majority one, to establish an embassy in Jerusalem. It is the fourth country to do so as of this writing. There are more promises we have received from other world leaders to move their embassies that have not happened yet. Brazil has made a vow to open an embassy in Jerusalem, but it does a great deal of trade in the Arab world. Predictably, its talk of the move received a great deal of pushback from Arab countries, but I feel certain Brazil will keep its promise. Another leader from an important African country has made a similar promise, and I feel sure he will honor his word. I understand the pressure that this and other countries receive from the Arab League and others, and I hope they have the courage to make the right decision. After all, they can see that the countries who have done it have been done no harm. The world keeps spinning, and life continues.

It is not just the work of convincing nations to move their embassies to Jerusalem that I pursued autonomously. I continued to act independently and behind the scenes nearly every day at the UN, out of necessity. Whenever I asked for guidance, the bureaucracy continued its efforts to discourage me from doing much of anything. But I didn't agree to move my family to New York so I could spend my time dining in fancy restaurants and attending cocktail parties. I came to work, to make progress on behalf of Israel, and strengthen our position in the world. I was able to work with countries with whom we had no diplomatic ties (although we have established ties with some of them more recently) to coordinate policy and promote mutually beneficial resolutions in the UN arena.

In 2017, we were able to promote a resolution against Hezbollah in Lebanon by working with other countries behind the scenes to make it happen. I would not take credit for it in public, because I knew this would create unwanted backlash that would overshadow and potentially undermine the effort.

The initiative to designate Hezbollah at the UN as a terrorist organization was important for Israel. Hezbollah operates from Lebanon, launches rockets and missiles on the border with Israel, and in doing so, poses a major threat to our security. Lebanon is a dysfunctional country and very weak politically. Hezbollah is the de facto leader of the country, and it uses the country as a base that will eventually be used to attack Israel. It's just a matter of time. The fact that we were able to convince other Arab countries to get on board with our resolution was remarkable. We reached a point where we had direct cooperation and discussions about this resolution and the language it would contain. We worked through the wording with several ambassadors in the region. Generally, the security council was hesitant or refused to name Hezbollah outright in any resolution condemning terror. It preferred generics such as "terror organization," "militias," or "group," because, otherwise, there would be tremendous opposition from some countries.

We wrote the resolution knowing that it would be difficult to get it passed as written. Indeed, it did not pass, because it was blocked by Russia and China, specifically because Hezbollah was named in it. During negotiations over the wording of the resolution, significant portions were removed that had direct reference to Hezbollah as conducting prohibited military activity in southern Lebanon, a violation of Resolution 1701. Russia insisted all mention of Hezbollah be omitted.[42]

This is nothing new. The UN has long been loath to call out Hezbollah by name. Oftentimes, UN language around Hezbollah and terror is watered down by Russia, sometimes by China, and often by both. In typical fashion, the UN Security Council usually issues statements that say such things as all Lebanese parties should "refrain from any involvement in the Syrian crisis."[43] While the UN issued many counterterrorism resolutions, it also has not

IN THE LION'S DEN

truly defined what terrorism is in any real way, which leaves room for individual states to collaborate with groups not specifically targeted or named by the UN. The UN can and has cracked down on specific groups in the past, so it absolutely has the power to do so. For instance, the UN Security Council has imposed sanctions on al Qaeda in several resolutions which go back to the late 1990s.[44] In a similar vein, the security council has the authority, if its members are willing, to target Hezbollah, but they do not do so because of pressure from Moscow and Beijing.

There is some momentum around the reality of Hezbollah that gave me some hope. The United States, the United Kingdom, Germany, the Arab League, and Israel officially recognize it in its entirely as a terrorist organization. In 2013, after hesitating for many years, France placed the organization on a list of terror groups. The European Union as a whole has been slower to take a stand; to date, it has designated only Hezbollah's military wing as a terror organization, a decision made in 2013, after the attack on a tourist bus outside the Burgas airport in Bulgaria in 2012. Still, the UN generally limits itself to ineffectual generic admonishments, which only encourage Hezbollah and its activities.

Yet I consider presenting the resolution a win. I brought forth a document that called Hezbollah what it was, a terror group, to the floor of the UN for the first time, despite skepticism from my colleagues. That was a success for us. We also exposed the problem of Lebanese Islamists and revealed those who back Hezbollah and excuse them. We managed this maneuver with the help of several Arab countries.

Many times, we saw China and Russia taking positions that were openly hostile to Israel, including many that were expressed in the security council, despite having strong bilateral relations with both of them. The most vocal is generally Russia, with China following its lead on issues having to do with the Middle East. For Russia, it is key to be influential mainly in the northern region, Syria and Lebanon. As part of Russia's support of the

Assad regime, they collaborated with militant groups, including Hezbollah. Russia sent what I would call a symbolic number of troops, a few thousand military police, to the region to show they are there and keeping watch. Strategically for Russia, they want to have a presence in the region to have access to a port in the Mediterranean, which they see as a strategic military location.

Since late 2015, Hezbollah has worked closely with the Russian military, which intervened in an attempt to save the Assad regime. Hezbollah's success as a military force in Syria has been endorsed by Moscow, which sees it as a useful and capable ally that has contributed to the survival of the Syrian government.[45] As for China, Lebanon sees the country as a potential economic savior.

One of the pursuits I was not successful with, but one that I pushed very hard for, was my bid for a seat for Israel on the security council. There are fifteen members on the council, five permanent members and ten rotating seats. The rotating seats serve two years, but there is an election every year for those seats. Each region presents candidates for the open seats, and often there is competition. In the African groups and the Arab League, there is generally no competition, but this is not the case for other regions. Israel wasn't part of any regional group until 2000, when, after fifty years, we joined the West European and Others Group (WEOG).[46]

Before this time, we were not in a position to run for a seat on the security council. Once we were in, it allowed us to think about running for positions. When we became a member of WEOG, we registered immediately to run for the security council. Many countries register years in advance to signal to other members of their group to pick another year to run.

Israel and Belgium were the only countries running in 2018. Unfortunately, Germany decided to step in, which is something we did not appreciate. Germany believes it should have a permanent seat, but because of the structure of the UN, this is not the case. If you look at their involvement in UN affairs when compared to France or the United Kingdom, Germany is right: it does

IN THE LION'S DEN

deserve to be in the room. As a result of not being a permanent member, Germany runs as often as it can. It was not collegial to Israel to run in 2018, because it was generally understood that if Germany ran, it would win.

Naturally, after Germany joined the race, there was internal debate in Israel whether we should stay in the race or not. Most of my colleagues at the Ministry of Foreign Affairs were especially skeptical about the race and recommended Israel not take the risk of running and losing. My feeling was that even if we lost, it would have been good to run. It would show people that we were willing to take the risk and put ourselves on the line for a role we believed we deserved to have. If we had won, it would have brought honor to Israel and given it exposure at the most important body of the UN. Running for such a seat would also serve us in the future. That's how I look at my entire career. You win some and you lose some, but in the process, you make your positions known. You show strength in the face of adversity, and you prove you're a fighter. I thought it was a mistake to withdraw.

I was aggressive about running for the seat. When I was back home in Israel, I insisted on seeing the prime minister in a one-on-one meeting to discuss the race. I knew he was getting pressure from the ministry of foreign affairs to back down. I was seeking his blessing to make the run. If we won that race, it would be historic, and it would happen under his leadership. Before my flight back to New York, I was called to a meeting at the prime minister's house. We sat on the porch, and in my experience, this was a good sign, because it showed me that the prime minister felt relaxed and had time to discuss the issue. I presented to him the importance of the campaign and what it could achieve, even if we lost. I knew how to talk to him, because I had so much experience in convincing him to make difficult or bold decisions in the past. A run would be a victory. A win would make him the first Israeli prime minister to make history at the UN. If we lost, I would take the heat. I had no problem with doing so, indeed I'd be proud to accept responsibility for a lost run, because it would be a good and meaningful effort that would be remembered. And next time, a win could be in the offing.

I told him to imagine arriving in New York and presiding over the security council. The impact we can make by sitting in the council for two years is unlimited. After an hour's discussion, he gave me the green light. It was a great moment. It was an important decision that could lead to major accomplishments, as it was when I ran for and won the chairmanship of the UN legal or Sixth Committee. I knew the people who opposed the race would try to constrain the campaign budget. I spoke immediately with the minister of finance, a friend, and explained the situation. He told me that for such an important cause they would find the money. We were on the right track. A few days later, it was heartening for me to watch the prime minister asking for support for the race at a public event in Asia.

I started to build the team and the plan for the campaign. Once I was back in Manhattan, however, a senior bureaucrat in the ministry of foreign affairs who worked closely with the prime minister and saw him a great deal, tried to convince him to drop out. He constantly claimed that the ministry was too weak, that there was not enough budget or manpower for such a race. I was not aware of this until later. A few months down the road, the prime minister made the decision to back out of the race.[47] I thought it was a bad idea, and privately, I stressed my opinion. There would be no humiliation in a loss. The prime minister listened to those around him when they told him any run should be put off for "a better timing." There is no such thing. All our important historical decisions took place when it was not the best timing. Backing out meant we closed the window for at least another decade. This was despite the fact that I had definitive commitments of support from ninety countries before we even launched the campaign.

I was disappointed and felt somewhat betrayed, not only that the bureaucrats were able to overcome and convince the prime minister to back down, but that they had the chutzpah to ask me to be the one to make the announcement that we were not running. The hypocrisy was stunning. In order to minimize the damage, I scheduled the announcement to go out on a late Friday afternoon, almost Shabbat in Israel, and when people in the US would be leaving for the weekend. I also had to deliver the news to our supporters in the UN, which was difficult. Many were as or more disappointed than I was.

There was a chance we could have won, and even if we didn't, running for such a seat would set a precedent and say something important about Israel, which is that we are willing to put ourselves on the line for what we believe in. We also would have made serious contributions as a seat holder on the security council. Once we decided to postpone it, many years would have to pass before we could identify another chance to run.

We put out the press release on a Friday afternoon. It was almost Shabbat in Israel, which meant no one would pay attention to the release. Still, I received many phone calls from ambassadors telling me they had the votes for Israel. One of them told me that he extended his stay at the UN to vote for us, that "no matter the instructions I would have received I would have voted for you guys, it's about time!" He was really upset with that decision. I told him that I appreciated his friendship, and I agreed it was a mistake to withdraw. Yes, it would have been challenging to beat Germany, but the run against Belgium would have been interesting. We might have won that seat, but we will never know. I guarantee that we would have put on an excellent campaign. Win or lose, Israel would have made an impression and showed the world that we do not wait for permission to take a stand or do something bold.

A win would have had such a huge upside, it was worth the risk of losing. We would have gained a certain amount of clout, which would have helped us become more closely involved with more issues. If given the chance, I would do it again. I advocate for my successors to start the years-long process to run again.

Acting even when there are those saying no takes courage, but it is one of the most effective ways to stand up to bullies. Let them know you are not easily intimidated and to say that you mean business. It's an important signal to supporters that they are not alone. It takes just one voice to encourage others to speak up.

All Wins Don't Look the Same

Wins can sometimes look like losses to outsiders. A resolution we brought to the floor of the UN against Hamas did not get the two-thirds majority required to pass, but we *did* get a majority of those voting in favor—eighty-seven voted in favor, fifty-eight voted against, with thirty-two abstentions.[48] The EU also supported the resolution condemning Hamas, and it was no easy task to get that support. Ambassador Haley and I worked hard to achieve its backing. I was also met with much skepticism over this resolution, and even though it lost due to UN voting rules, I consider it a win because it created an opening for future resolutions that I believe will pass. We also now have a more open dialogue about terror groups with the EU.

The plurality vote was impressive, and we were proud of the effort. Because of bold decisions, acting autonomously, and showing convictions, more and more countries are now open to publicly supporting Israel. Many of these countries have worked and negotiated with us privately, but they are now willing to be public about it, because we show we are not reticent to act without permission or the blessing of outsiders. That is a show of strength, not recklessness.

CHAPTER SIX

Prepare for all Eventualities

*Seeing around corners and preparing
for them is a must.*

The hallmark of security is the ability to see around corners and be ready for what is there before making the turn. Applying the knowledge gained from experience is crucial to the ability to take quick action. This is true in any form of decision-making, negotiations, reaching stated goals, and in military action and defense, especially when you live in a tough neighborhood. If you plan to take a walk alone after dark, in a crime-ridden area of town, don't you think about the route you will use and the precautions you'll take to protect yourself from harm? No one would criticize you for doing so; indeed, they may wonder about your sanity if you were careless and did not consider your safety before venturing out in such a circumstance. However, Israel is criticized time[49] and again[50] for its preparation and strategic planning in an ongoing effort to stop attacks from happening in the first place and putting an end to attacks when they do happen.[51] It is necessary, therefore, not only to prepare for violence, but to also prepare for the inevitable fallout we face from critics every time we defend ourselves.

In late 2018, we exposed terror tunnels on the border with Lebanon[52] and neutralized them using a combination of military strategy and diplomacy. It was a major turn of events to discover these tunnels, because had they been used, a major war on the border would have broken out. Let me be clear. These were not primitive, underground trenches. They were sophisticated, lined routes equipped with electricity and air conditioning. We had to ensure that terrorists could not use them to access communities on the Israeli side.

Hezbollah's construction of a network of tunnels into Israel was a top-secret operation; even the organization's top officers on the ground were unaware of it. Funding had been provided by Iran. The tunnels would allow hundreds of special elite Hezbollah forces to assume control of communities near the border on the Israeli side. The plan included kidnapping residents back into Lebanon and conducting a ground fight with Israeli troops, who would naturally have to come into the area. The terrorists' aim was to take hold of a community, raise a Hezbollah flag, and claim they had seized the area. This would give Hezbollah a chance to broadcast the entire operation live and claim credit for "conquering the northern part of Israel."

We used a combination of intelligence resources to gather data and pinpoint where the tunnels had been constructed. A week before the day we planned to start the operation, the Israeli military attaché had come from the Washington embassy to brief me on the issue. He showed me the location of the tunnels and what the operation to destroy the tunnels on the Israeli side would look like.

We knew once we started drilling on the Israeli side to destroy the tunnels, our intentions would be exposed, with three possible responses. In scenario A, Hezbollah would attack the engineers drilling and the residential communities in the area, which could ignite an all-out war. Hezbollah has the capability to launch tens of thousands of rockets and missiles into Israel. This would require a military response from Israel and lead to weeks of bloody confrontation. Scenario B would be less dramatic. There would be some fighting at the border, but the violence would be contained quickly. In scenario C, Hezbollah would see what we were doing but would not respond to it. We had to be ready for all three. We didn't know which response Hezbollah would choose once we started to destroy the tunnels; not doing so was not an option.

Preparation was challenging because you have to be ready for the potential of full war without exposing too many people so that our assumptions and plans were known only to those who needed to know. I prepared as much intelligence as I could on the tunnel construction. It's valuable to declassify some carefully chosen intelligence, because revealing information affords tremendous leverage. Even after we started drilling, in order for Israel to be successful in getting support, we had to convince our allies, fellow diplomats, and other countries that the activities we were engaged in were justified because of potential threats. I started to prepare the diplomatic front. I knew that when I discussed the measures we were taking to neutralize the tunnels with an official on the UN security council, I would show him classified information that clearly shows aerial photographs of tunnels beneath UN facilities. It's not just Israel that is under threat; there could be devastating consequences for UN peacekeepers if Hezbollah's aggressions go unanswered. Once officials see with their own eyes what is going on, they tend to adopt our position and support it.

There is always a healthy tension between diplomats and military intelligence, especially when it comes to declassifying information. The military's first reaction is not to declassify information at all. They must consider the risk of exposing our sources. They claim that the risks to them increases when information is made public. I served as the deputy minister of defense. During my appointment, I developed close ties with many in the military and the ministry of defense, and I have personal relationships with many of them. I was able to convince the chief of staff of the military, Gadi Eizenkot, of the strategic importance of the declassification process. Having proprietary information in hand brought people to our side. This information allowed us to score valuable points with important international leaders and improve our position with the international media, which is usually hostile to us. Some of the information that was declassified would become public over time, but having it first and being able to show it to key players was crucial in fighting backlash for our necessary actions.

In the case of the tunnels, we knew we were going to drill only on our side, and we were able to show senior members of the security council that the tunnels did in fact start in Lebanon and exactly where they penetrated Israel. Once you demonstrate reality based on precise intelligence, and they can see Hezbollah is violating all UN decisions and hiding behind UN facilities to dig the tunnels in the ground, it's hard to argue against our preventive activities. Part of my vision for the security of Israel is that it is not enough to win on the battleground; we also have to win the hearts and minds of the world. Each time we have to defend ourselves, we must remember we are fighting on three fronts—on the ground, diplomatically, and with public opinion.

It takes a lot of energy from the system to review material to be declassified, but it is part of preparation to assure the legitimacy of acts of self-defense. If someone argues against us even after seeing the evidence, we will go forward with confidence. In this case, there could be no question about our necessity to act. If someone didn't want to see it, that would be their problem; I was confident I laid out our position and reasoning.

We shared our plans with a small number of critical people at the US UN mission, reassuring them that the activities on the ground, which involved engineering and heavy machinery, would be done *only* on our side of the border, with the work on our side of tunnels itself completed by highly trained and sophisticated civilian engineers. Before the drilling started, I prepared materials such as maps, diagrams, and aerial photos of entry points to the tunnels to emphasize that some of the tunnel locations were directly under UN facilities. I was now set to meet with

My father,
Joseph Danon.

My father Joseph Danon with my mother Yocheved Danon touring Israel before my father was wounded in the War of Attrition.

Organizing my first large-scale event for Jewish students in Florida with honorary speaker PM Yitzchak Shamir, 1993

Credit: Personal photo library

Meeting my dear friend Elie Wiesel, blessed be his memory, in his office in New York, 2015

Credit: Personal photo library

Presenting my credentials to the secretary general of the UN,
Ban Ki-moon, at the UN headquarters, November 2015

Marking 40 years since UN resolution 3379, which equated zionism to racism.
The resolution was repealed in 1991. In the picture from right to left, Michael
Herzog, Isaac Herzog, Secretary Kerry, S.G. Ban Ki-moon, myself, Amb. Samantha
Power and David Harris. November, 2015

Memorial event at the UN for former Israeli President Shimon Peres, with S.G. Ban Ki-moon and Amb. Samantha Power, September 2016

With Amb. Samantha Power and Amb. Daniel Shapiro during a tour of Israel's Southern border.

My first meeting with Amb. Nikki Haley at the Israeli mission in New York. Amb. Haley chose to disregard protocol and advanced her meeting with me, March 2017

Credit: Personal photo library

Discussing the mechanism of UN reports in a meeting with S.G Guterres.

Credit: Personal photo library

Together with Amb. Nikki Haley at the Kerem Shalom border crossing with Gaza. Also in the picture Deputy Chief of General Staff of the IDF, Aviv Kochavi and senior advisor to Amb. Haley, Jon Lerner. June 2017

Credit: Matty Stern/U.S. Embassy Jerusalem

Touring the Hamas terror tunnels with Amb. Nikki Haley during her visit to Israel, June 2017

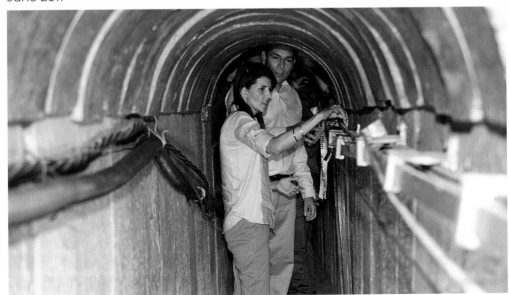

Credit: Matty Stern/U.S. Embassy Jerusalem

Entering the presidential residence of Reuven Rivlin with Amb. Nikki Haley, June 2017

Credit: Matty Stern/U.S. Embassy Jerusalem

Selfie on a helicopter ride touring Israel with (left to right) Ambs. of Kenya, Australia and Gabon, July 2017

Credit: Personal photo library

Presiding over a General Assembly session at the UN in my role as Vice President of the General Assembly, September 2017

Congratulating President Trump after his first speech at the UN General Assembly, September 2017

Presiding over the UN General Assembly during a speech by PM Netanyahu, 2017

Credit: Shahar Azran

Press briefing at the UN ahead of a Security Council meeting, October 2017

Credit: UN Photo/Kim Haughton

With VP Mike Pence at the reenactment of the UN partition plan vote. At the Queen's Museum, New York, November 2017

Presenting an ancient coin which proves our eternal connection to Jerusalem, December 2017

Addressing the General Assembly of the UN.

Greeting President Rivlin on his arrival to New York. With my wife Talie, my son Aviad and my two daughters Hila and Shira.

Bringing Judaism to the UN. Passover seder with my ambassadorial colleagues. Pictured with the Amb. of Rwanda, March 2018

Credit: Personal photo library

With S.G Antonio Guterres during a traditional Tashlich Ceremony before Yom Kippur, September 2018

Credit: UN Photo/Evan Schneider

Delivering the "Bible Speech" at the UN Security Council. The speech which stressed our eternal rights to the land of Israel went viral on social media.

Credit: UN Photo/Evan Schneider

Credit: Personal photo library

Last minute discussions before the opening of a security council meeting. With S.G. Antonio Guterres and President Macron, 2018

Credit: Personal photo library

Chairing the Sixth (Legal) Committee in the presence of the President of the General Assembly. My election set a precedent as the first Israeli ever to chair a UN Committee.

Leading the March of the Living at the gates of Auschwitz, Poland, with a UN Ambassadorial delegation, March 2019

A spontaneous visit with a delegation of UN Ambassadors to the site of a rocket attack in Ashkelon. In the picture, speaking with the Mayor of Ashkelon, Tomer Glam, May 2019

In the TV studio at FOX News for an interview with Lou Dobbs, 2019

Credit: Personal photo library

Sharing the story of Israel's pioneering technologies with the African Ambassadors. At the Bergman's residence in New York, 2019

Credit: Personal photo library

The best way to understand Israel is to visit Israel. In the picture with one of the UN Ambassadorial delegations at the Western Wall.

Credit: Eyal Eliyahu

Briefing UN Ambassadors with PM Benjamin Netanyahu before our helicopter tour of the Northern border of Israel.

Participating in an event at the Dubai Expo by invitation of the UAE government, October 2021

ambassadors. Only a few people from the US administration were informed in advance about the operation. Even my staff was told very little. I couldn't even tell my wife.

There was no sleep for me on the evening of the operation. I thought back to the time when I was taking the IDF officer's course during the Gulf War in the 1990s. We were deployed into Gaza and were on high alert. Rockets were flying from Iraq continuously. As a result, we would sleep in our shoes and uniform, ready to respond in a matter of minutes. The night of the drilling operation, I went to sleep on similar high alert, but this time, I wore my suit and tie.

It was almost midnight on December 4, 2018 on the East Coast when the Operation Northern Shield[53] started in the early morning hours in Israel. Tensions were high in the IDF headquarters in Tel Aviv and in our offices in New York, as we thought about what the reaction would be. Some of them would be predictably incendiary and critical, but we had no doubt we were in the right. The drilling along the border between Israel and Lebanon began simultaneously and stretched from the Mediterranean Sea to the east, near Mount Hermon. This was challenging choreography because Hezbollah watched the border closely. We disguised the machinery and the engineers. We breathed a bit more freely only when Hezbollah issued a press release claiming that the tunnels were fake, and that Israel was lying about them. Evidence proved otherwise, but the press release meant Hezbollah was embarrassed. When they put that statement out, I knew I could sleep for a few hours. It meant they were not taking responsibility for the tunnels. They said it was a lie, so in effect, they chose scenario C and ignored what we were doing. This meant it would be quiet and we could complete the job. They claimed to have nothing to do with the tunnels, and there were no hostile activities in response. No rockets flew into Israel.

The next morning, it was a diplomatic marathon of meetings for me. We called all ambassadors in the security council, but this time I could not call and schedule a meeting in advance. I have a personal relationship with most of them, so I opted to send each of them a text message explaining that I had to see them as soon as possible, at home, in their office, or even for a brief meeting outside of the security council itself. I needed fifteen minutes. I ran from mission to mission with all the maps and information we had prepared. I shared all the information I could before it was released to the media. I explained how the tunnels were constructed and about the actions we took on our side. There was some talk of either blowing up the tunnels or filling them with high-pressure cement. Because this type of material would come out on the other side of the border, our legal advisers said it would be a violation of international law to go this route. As a result, we made sure all of our activities were on our side of the fence. We blocked part of the tunnels with cement and demolished the portion of the tunnels in Israel with explosives.

A few days after the operation, we had a debate about the tunnels in the security council. We absolutely won support for the operation, including from France, who can be very difficult. This was early in December 2018. I was able to show maps and photos of the tunnels and prove not only that the tunnels were real, but that Hezbollah had clearly violated Resolution 1701, a 2006 UN resolution that ended the thirty-four-day war between Hezbollah and Israel, called for the demilitarization of southern Lebanon, and reaffirmed past calls for the disarmament of Hezbollah.

For the sake of the people of Lebanon, I said, the country had to act against Hezbollah. Once Israel is forced to defend itself, it will be the Lebanese people who will pay the price. If such a major attack becomes necessary, we will not hesitate to bury Hezbollah under the ruins of Lebanon. In other words, I made it clear that we would do what is necessary to protect our people. As I spoke, I looked directly at the Lebanese ambassador, Amal Mudallali. Even though we were not friends, I knew she was listening. She knew what our retaliation would mean for her people, but she was, in a sense, held hostage by Hezbollah. She seemed to have little will to stand against it.

Ultimately, we exposed the tunnels publicly to show the real intentions of Hezbollah. We sealed all of them off but one. At the border on the Israeli side, we left part of the tunnel intact to demonstrate how it and the others were constructed. I brought a group of ambassadors to the area to show them. They could see for themselves the air conditioning system, electric lights, and the magnitude of the structure's width and length. This one remaining tunnel has become a useful reminder of what really happens on the border, and why we must prepare and be ready to defend the line. Bad things happen when you look the other way and forget to do your homework.

Own the Narrative

When the US moved its embassy from Tel Aviv to Jerusalem, we expected there would be pushback from the Palestinians. We knew there would probably be riots at the fence between Gaza and Israel. Groups like Hamas generally incite such disruptions, to take attention from anything positive about Israel. The tragic part about this is that there are always casualties that are avoidable had riots not been incited. The organization also recognizes that the more casualties there are on their side, the more press coverage they will receive. Our intention is always to minimize casualties while our enemy's goal is to increase the number.

Before the day of the move arrived, Israel announced clearly that anyone who approached the fence on that day or the days leading up to the opening ceremony would be considered a terrorist and would be dealt with as such. The rioting terrorists at the border, some fifty miles away from the location of the embassy, hurled firebombs and explosive devices toward the security fence and IDF forces. They threw burning rubber tires over the fence, along with other flaming objects and rocks, as a way of igniting fires in Israeli territory and harming Israeli troops. Experience has shown the riot organizers that Israel does not stand still when such events take place. We are prepared and we act.

There were casualties. Palestinian reports put the figure close to fifty-eight killed and nearly three thousand injured among the rioters and terrorists.[54] It was a challenge for us because one fatality was a young boy, the other was an older man in a wheelchair holding a slingshot. It is unfortunate that Hamas terrorists use innocent civilians as human shields. They hide behind civilians, women, and children. It is problematic, because they know full well that casualties are inevitable. We were able to gather intelligence that major parts of the organizers were Hamas terrorists. Their plan was to break the fence together with the mob that gathered there and enter Israel to commit terror attacks. Once the fence is breached, you have no control over who is entering and what they are bringing with them. It was not a spontaneous demonstration of civilians. It was a terrorist-organized and -run event.

We knew the media would show photographs and videos of the riots, which took attention away from the ceremony in Jerusalem. The UN Security Council had a moment of silence for the casualties of the riots when they met the following morning, and that decision was made without notifying us. I learned about this a minute before entering the security council chamber, and I instructed my staff not to enter until that show was over. I didn't want to be part of it and be in the room and stand knowing the majority of those people were terrorists.

Many victims were young people. Hamas controlled the narrative, and the international media complied by portraying a false narrative that we were shooting civilians who were protesting. It was nothing of the sort. We were dealing with terrorists taking advantage of innocent people. I decided we had to analyze the victims one by one. To do that, we received the support of our colleagues in the intelligence and military. Each has a database and the capability to identify who the Palestinians were and to find links between them and terror groups. Oftentimes their names were openly and proudly reported in the Palestinian press. We can see who was arrested as a terrorist or paid a salary by Hamas to engage in terrorism. After we completed the analysis, we found that in fact the majority of the victims were involved with Hamas and paid by Hamas. We proved our case that they were not innocent civilians, but terrorists exploiting the embassy event to launch a campaign against us.

This is important work to do, as it puts events like this in perspective. Once people see the numbers and realize that the majority of the people rioting were part of Hamas or paid by Hamas and involved in terror activities, our actions and their outcome can be better understood.

I came to the next security council meeting ready with the research we had prepared. It was crucial to be able to prove that the moment of silence was not for "innocents," but for terrorists. It was effective. Those in the hall who were against the embassy move (and there were many, including the ambassadors from Bolivia and the Arab countries) also did not want to be associated with Hamas. While they would like to defend "innocent teens," when they see clearly that those people were connected to terrorism, they must go on the defense, and do so publicly. I was able to work with information we had prepared to make a solid case that these were not innocent young protesters on the fence. I shared the information with the security council, saying the name of each and every terrorist who was killed and identifying their affiliation with Hamas. Many of the people in the room didn't feel comfortable. A few days before, they had their moment of silence. It's one thing when you stand up to show solidarity with innocent teenagers killed in a demonstration, but when you reveal the fact that they were terrorists, it's not pleasant, nor should it be.

Participate to Advance

Political maneuvers and strategy also require planning. I believe Israel can be a member of every body of the UN. When I decided to run for a chairmanship of a committee, it was considered impossible, and some in Israel even thought I was aiming too high. The campaign for the chairmanship of the Sixth Committee required quiet planning and many discreet meetings to gather support. This level of groundwork is one of the skills I brought with me from Israeli politics. When you work with people, it is always the same; you build friendships and you make sure that your friends will gain leverage from your victories. My main point was it will not be my victory, it will be yours; once I head the committee, things will be much better for you and your country.

The general assembly has six standing committees that report to it: disarmament, economic and financial issues, human rights, decolonization, the UN budget, and legal issues. The Legal Committee, or Sixth Committee, oversees issues related to international law. There was absolutely no reason why Israel cannot chair this or any other committee. After we joined WEOG, we became eligible to present our candidacy for different positions, but we never put it to a test by trying to win the chairmanship of a committee.

What was interesting about my election to the Sixth Committee is that normally committee heads are elected by voice consensus, and without a formal vote. But nothing is ever normal at the UN when it comes to Israel. Our opponents insisted upon a vote. The call led to a rebuke from the deputy US ambassador to the UN, David Pressman. "Even a chair from (former leader Muammar) Gaddafi's Libya was elected by acclamation," he said in a statement. "A vote should not have been called today. We need a United Nations that includes Israel, that brings Israel closer, not one that systematically pushes Israel away," he said. When I learned that there would be an opening for the position of chairmen of the six committees, I entered into election mode. Everyone who runs for any position finds enormous energy to do so—it's an emotional and intellectual high that is like no other. We can work days with very little sleep and stay sharp and focused to win the race. While it was not my first race, it was the first time I had run a campaign at the UN. It would also be a first for Israel. There was a lot on the line.

The first stage was to learn the bylaws and the rules of the game. I figured out that I had to secure the support of our regional group. It was a chess game. Once the Palestinians learned about my efforts, they would do everything possible to prevent it from happening. I called my senior staff together, told them to drop all their assignments, and over the next four hours simulate working against Israel on this issue. This is a technique I learned in the military that helps anticipate enemy action, known as enemy simulation. I wanted to know all the possible arguments against us sitting on the committee and everything the Palestinians and their allies would use to try and block my nomination and appointment. "Don't omit even the most radical steps," I said. The harder we worked before our goal became public, the better our chances were to win.

One of the conclusions we came to was that the Palestinians would first try to block us from receiving the support of the group, since it would be easier for them to find another member state to compete with us in the group rather than block us in the general assembly. Once we analyzed the list of WEOG members, we realized that the Palestinians would likely push either Turkey or Malta to present a nomination. After I quietly gathered the support from our allies, I went to meet with the ambassadors from these countries and made sure they would not present their candidacy after I presented mine.

After I received the confirmation, I called our legal advisor and I told him to submit my application. As expected, our adversaries were not quiet. They tried to find a way to block me in WEOG, but by then, it was too late. I gathered the support of the majority of the group. We passed the first stage. The Palestinian representative made a statement that my nomination would be blocked in the general assembly. He should have read my biography before making such a claim, as he would have learned that I had a very extensive experience in gathering support and winning elections. I kept quiet and instructed my team to not to respond to any media inquiry until after the vote.

While the other side ran a nasty campaign against my nomination, claiming that Israel could not possibly sit or chair such an important committee because we "violate international law," I invested my time in personal meetings with ambassadors. Many of them did not know me yet, so it was a great way to make new friends. The week before the vote, Iran tried to lead the G-77 group to issue a letter against my nomination. If such a letter was issued, it could create the impression that the majority of the member states did not support us, which was not the case.

According to the procedures of the G-77, once the chairman of the group sent a draft letter, and there is no public opposition to the letter, it becomes the group position. Iran was chairing the group that year and took advantage of it. I knew we had a problem. The vote in the general assembly would be in secret ballots, which would allow many to vote for me without receiving any heat from the Palestinians and the Arab League. However, to block the Iranian initiative, one must also send a public letter to the entire group and expose support for my nomination.

Time was of an essence; it was just a few hours before the deadline. I received a call from my friend, the Ambassador of Singapore, Burhan Gafoor. He informed me that he had received approval to send his rejection of the letter. I was afraid that Iran would ignore Singapore and submit the original letter to all member states anyway. Only after both India and Rwanda issued a public statement against the Iranian initiative that I knew we had successfully blocked the maneuver.

The day of the vote was like a festival at the UN. Everyone loves an election, especially one with so much tension around it. Everybody showed up, and I was ready for the vote. I knew I had the votes, the only question was, would an attempt to postpone it work? I went over all the scenarios with my team. We were more than ready. When the debate started, many countries from the Organization of Islamic Countries (OIC) took the podium to attack me. I was laughing to myself that I was the only one who knew how many votes we were actually going to receive from that group. The attacks were harsh on me personally and against Israel. The representative from Norway approached me and said that many members of WEOG would like to counter the attacks and speak before the vote. I replied politely but firmly, "No way, no one speaks before." She did not understand at the time. I had the votes. I learned from many debates and meetings that when you have the numbers, you start the vote. I did not want any delays; we could always speak after the vote.

After all the speakers against us finished, we began the vote. Each ambassador had to write his or her choice on a slip of paper and enter it into the ballot. The Palestinian representative was smiling. I was worried that maybe something went wrong. Even though when I looked around and read the faces of my colleagues, I knew that the majority was with me, it was still a tense few minutes. Anything can happen.

I called my wife and asked her to bring our children to the hall, even though voting was not yet completed. I had done my best, and I was very proud of myself, my team, and the many friends from all around the world who helped me.

The president of the assembly announced the results. I received the support of 109 member states. Only forty-four voted against me.

Israel won the chair. It was the first time Israel chaired one of the world body's six permanent committees since joining the UN in 1949. In chairing the committee, I was able to give Israel a higher profile in procedural dealings at the UN. Since Israel is a world leader in international law and fighting terrorism, I brought direct experience in both of these to the table. I was quite happy for the opportunity to share our knowledge about these subjects with other ambassadors.

The chief Palestinian delegate at the United Nations, Riyad Mansour, predictably complained about my election to the chairmanship, telling reporters that Arab and Muslim countries had tried to prevent the win. He accused us of being "the biggest violator of international law" and predicted I would threaten the work of the Sixth Committee. He was wrong. In chairing the committee in a respectful, professional, and effective manner, I proved that there is no reason why Israel cannot serve in any position at the UN. It can be and should be.

Making the Case

In diplomacy and politics, you must always convince people of your views so you can achieve your goals. I did this in both arenas. In 2013, I was elected to become chairman of the Likud party's central committee, which is the most important body of the party. It consists of three thousand elected officials from different parts of Israel. Conventions are held, but in the Likud, there is a central committee where the most important or senior people in the party meet to decide on crucial positions in the party. These positions represent all branches from north to the south.

Whenever there was an ideological dispute with the prime minister, who is the chairman of the party, we had to bring it to a vote to the central committee. I was leading the opposition to a building freeze in Judea and Samaria that the prime minister orchestrated after receiving a great deal of pressure from President Obama. I knew that I could win only if the ballots were secret. In order to make it happen, I collected the required signatures. Once that was done, it was expected that I would have the majority. Had the vote been public, the prime minister would have won, because people do not want to show what could be perceived as disloyalty to him in public.

Prime Minister Netanyahu also knew he would lose in a secret ballot, so he tried to impose an open vote. What happened next was remarkable. Hundreds of people shouted, demanding secret ballots. In the past, he would come, give his speech, and there would be a show of hands for any decision he wanted. He would have the majority and it would be done. With hundreds demanding secret ballots, there was nothing else to do but give them what they asked for. Once he realized he could not do it, he postponed that vote.

Prime Minister Netanyahu would often ask me how I was able to capture the majority of votes in the central committee; he could not understand it. I told him that everything we did was well-thought out and planned. We made sure our positions were clear and delivered in advance to our people. I was honest about what I wanted to achieve and what I believed. My people knew exactly where I stood all the time, even if it necessitated confronting the prime minister about an idea or policy.

After he closed the meeting, Prime Minister Netanyahu called me to his car to explain to him what happened and why so many were shouting. My position is that even if we clash over ideology, I will be polite, and not go after him personally. You can be strong and direct without resorting to ad hominem attacks. I told him it was not personal against him, but that as a leader, he must also listen to others. I earned their trust. It was not that they were against the prime minister per se. My win was a surprise to many, but I had become accustomed to being underestimated by both colleagues and adversaries.

My disagreements were never against the prime minister as a person, but strictly ideological. Unfortunately, he often took this personally.

Despite the opposition from his party, the prime minister agreed to the US demand for the freeze. There was additional pressure from the US to extend this timeframe, and the prime minister was inclined to agree. I was solidly against this, to both the ten-month freeze and the extension, and I was able to gather support at the party level against it. I was clear and public about it,

I said out loud what I meant before the vote. People knew I would not compromise, including those who sometimes tire of politics. Even the most politically jaded knew that once I did my homework, I would make a commitment and have a stated goal. I would not go back on my word. This gave me strength and power, and that is why I was successful even when I had to stand against the prime minister.

There was another point at which I disagreed with Prime Minister Netanyahu, when we responded to serious fighting in Gaza. At the time, I was the deputy minister of defense. On June 12, 2014, three Israeli teenagers, Eyal Yifrach, Gilad Shaar, and Naftali Frenkel were kidnapped by Hamas. It was an emotional time for the entire country who was waiting to hear their fate. Many citizens volunteered to search for the boys. They had been kidnapped on a Friday afternoon as they hitchhiked back home from their yeshiva. I went to visit the three families on Saturday night. I already knew that they had likely been kidnapped.

What we did not know at the time was whether they were alive. One of the boys had called from the car they had been pulled into. The police had a record of the call, and the information from it did not paint an optimistic picture. The boys represented three different families with three different backgrounds. Unfortunately, the boys were all murdered very shortly after they were taken. That event led to more violence. Once we started arresting Hamas operatives in Judea and Samaria, they began shooting rockets into Israel. We found ourselves in another round of violence. We also discovered that Hamas had tunnels that penetrated into Israel. These were not the same as Hezbollah's tunnels, they were less sophisticated. Still, they can be used to bring terrorists into the country, and it was a strategic threat to us. My position was that we cannot have a ceasefire with Hamas without first dealing with the threat of these tunnels.

At the time, US Secretary of State John Kerry was pushing Prime Minister Netanyahu for an immediate ceasefire. This was wrong for two reasons. First, we wanted them to pay a heavy price for shooting rockets. Second, if you accept a ceasefire and you have not dealt with the threat of the tunnels, you are still exposed to the threat. I told the prime minister that we should not accept the ceasefire before we neutralize the tunnels. I told him if he agrees to the pressure from the US, I would not stay on as the deputy minister of defense. It was a dilemma for me, because I knew that the prime minister had every intention to fire me. My advisors told me the right thing to do publicly was to resign before he announced it so I could get public support. In this situation, I didn't care about winning points. I was interested in the substance of what a ceasefire meant under these circumstances.

I knew that the prime minister cares about how things look in the public eye. Maybe it was a mistake, but I decided not to resign but to say publicly that I was against the ceasefire and that I would not stay in government. The prime minister let it leak to the press that he wanted to fire me and that my criticism did not support the efforts he was making. He was very vicious in his arguments.

After the prime minister removed me from my post, I was undeterred. I released a statement that read, "The prime minister doesn't accept that there are other views in his party. Netanyahu has this morning agreed to a ceasefire that was very bad for Israel."

I was able to work with him afterward despite the words he used, because I always look at the big picture. After he fired me, the cabinet approved the ceasefire, which was a bad decision. I felt Hamas was setting the conditions for us, which I rejected then and now. Ultimately, Hamas decided not to accept the ceasefire, and the Israeli government then did exactly what I demanded it do: continue the operation and neutralize the threat of the tunnels.

After this, the Likud Central Committee members who live in southern Israel were also becoming frustrated and angry at having to bear the brunt of Hamas terrorism while getting little attention and tepid responses from the government.

I wanted to have a meeting in the southern city of Ashkelon for the central committee to show solidarity with the people of the south. The prime minister was against it in part because he would have faced some very heavy criticism at the meeting. He told the party not to give me a budget, and some of his people tried to sabotage the preparation of the event. I planned the meeting myself, as I knew thousands of people would come to the conference. We sent out invitations, and I personally called the hotel where the meeting would be held. I told the manager that I would take full responsibility for the costs, and that he would be paid in full, despite letters he received from the party not to host the conference. I gave him my personal credit card for a security deposit. Still, party officials continued to try to stop the event.

Once he understood that I was determined to hold the event, the prime minister actually decided to hold an event at the same time and day in another city in central Israel. Two events at the same time. People had to choose which to attend. The media sent crews to both places. I planned everything carefully, organized it to the last detail, and included a resolution about supporting the people in the south and condemning Hamas and its violence. I brought in a senior member of the party to speak. Our meeting was a huge success, because more people showed up for it than they did for the prime minister's meeting. I had laid the groundwork and let people know what would be discussed, and what position I took regarding defending our communities. We voted for a resolution. It was a clear sign that when it came to ideology, I was willing to go all the way. When I left the venue that evening, one of the respected and elderly members of the party from Ashkelon told me that because the event was not canceled, he could still remain a proud member of the Likud party. If I had won one vocal convert, I knew I had won other silent ones.

I proved that we don't need long stretches of time to prepare for important events. Often, things must happen fast, and planning well and quickly comes from a mindset: What do we need to do to accomplish something? Let's do it. While you cannot do anything without preparation, it does not have to take a long time. Because of my experience organizing large gatherings in Israel, I was not afraid to use the UN as a platform for large-scale meetings. My young energetic team had become very adept at planning mega-events quickly, whether it was an anti-BDS event, an event celebrating the fiftieth year of the reunification of Jerusalem, or the reenactment of the historic vote to establish the state of Israel in Queens. These large-scale gatherings demonstrated we were capable. There were not many UN delegations who were capable of putting together such happenings. I had the courage and vision— and the will. I was often told, great idea, let's do it next year. I always said, let's do it now, we can get it done in two months.

I did the same planning when it came to hosting ambassadors on trips to Israel. Everything was planned in advance: every meeting, every visit to historical sites, to the tunnels, and to the border. We knew who the ambassadors would meet and what they would say. Nothing was left to chance, which resulted in a fun visit for my guests and an effective one for us. Planning, knowing, seeing what's next—these are important because Israel is not in a position to be taken off guard. Because we are a small country with so many enemies and challenges, we have narrow room for mistakes. Expert planning is crucial in every action we take.

CHAPTER SEVEN

Israel Must Play Offense

Calling out hypocrisy, wrongdoing,
unfair or unbalanced criticism, and
factual errors is a necessity.

I never hesitate to say good things about colleagues, but I'm also not reluctant to call out anyone who unfairly criticizes or libels Israel. We cannot let misrepresentations become engraved in the public record or popular opinion. Yes, it's an uphill battle on many fronts, especially at the UN and in much of the international community. There is a great deal of conflict and misunderstanding that is rooted in false information. It requires an offense strategy, which is not a problem for me. Offense wins the game.

As I've said on many occasions, I came to the UN from the Israeli parliament, where people, like many in political and business settings, publicly say good things about you; but behind closed doors, they can change their tone. At the UN, it's exactly the opposite—people are quite happy to publicly denounce Israel, but behind closed doors, they appreciate and admire us. What ambassadors do in public at the UN is often for show, but that doesn't mean it's any less dangerous. In order to minimize hypocrisy and double standards, there must be a price tag attached. It's the most effective way to get those who are quick to blast Israel to think twice before doing so. Holding people publicly accountable for their words and actions forces them to measure future statements and activities more carefully.

As I have mentioned, I've had to publicly call out the French ambassador on more than one[55] occasion at the UN, using the word "shameful" in doing so, when describing his stand on Israel.[56] This is despite the fact that it's not common protocol to name specific countries and ambassadors when addressing the security council. When I received information that the ambassador of France was working on a draft resolution condemning Israel for using excessive force when we had to block the riots and restore order, I did not speak in general about European countries or the EU. I named him in the address I gave to the UN Security Council discussing the issue. I responded to the French initiative, which called for stationing international observers on the Temple Mount, Judaism's holiest site, and said, "Israel will not agree to an international presence on the Temple Mount. If the international community wishes to be constructive, it should focus on ending the incitement.[57] No nation represented in this chamber would accept the presence of international forces in their capital."

When the idea of sending international observers to Jerusalem was brought up again, I went on the offense: I looked directly at the French ambassador and told him that I have seen how the French authorities dealt with the Yellow Vest demonstrations and riots in France. I said, "I don't recall anyone in this chamber criticizing your security forces when they use a lot of force to contain the riots. Maybe we should discuss sending international observers to the streets of Paris?"

"We know that your country wants to see peace in our region. We too want peace, but the only way to peace is with direct talks between the parties," I said in closing, still looking him straight in the eyes.

The French ambassador was bothered by the fact that I pointed to him; he was not accustomed to being addressed directly in such forums. Ambassadors assume that their words and actions will be politely ignored in public and only brought up discreetly and in private, away from the public glare. So naturally, it came as a shock to him that I noticed what he was doing and mentioned it aloud, in public. Now, there are new rules at the UN. I insisted on implementing my zero-tolerance approach: If you attack us, expect an immediate sharp response. It will be public and shameful for anyone who did not check the facts, for I will expose their lies. I changed the way things were done at the UN with this regarding Israel. During my term, such bashing was called out immediately and in the same venue where it was made. An added bonus: I would go to the media directly afterward to discuss it.

The French ambassador came to me after the meeting, and said, "It's not me. I'm just following instructions from my capital." This is an excuse I heard quite frequently at the UN. It's usually a lie. I told him that I knew that he was personally instrumental in crafting the language of the resolution condemning Israel. He did not want me to know this, but I did—and I was not going to pretend not to know for the sake of diplomacy. After a few times calling out the French ambassador in the media, not only did he reiterate that he did not appreciate it, which had no effect on me, but more importantly, it made him much more careful in the words he used and actions he took going forward. The language around Israel used by this and other ambassadors did not change completely. But they did choose their words more carefully going forward.

No Solidarity with Hatred, or Terrorists

The UN also holds an annual Day of Solidarity with the Palestinian People in late November. This is essentially an anti-Israel event, which generally features several anti-Israeli resolutions. It changes nothing on the ground and does not improve the lives of any Palestinian, but it does stir up hatred and resentment. At the 2016 event, I found myself calling out then-General Assembly

President Peter Thomson for censure, after he wore a scarf with the colors of the Palestine Liberation Organization (PLO) flag to an official session. "It's unacceptable for the president of the U.N. General Assembly, whose position is a symbol of neutrality and stateliness, to wrap himself in a Palestinian flag and participate in an event whose sole purpose is to attack and besmirch the state of Israel," I told the gathering.[58] In fact, each year the event was held, I had to clearly make my position known that the event was disingenuous at the very least, and dangerously inciteful at its worst.

The UN has also tried to cloak terrorists in the respectability of its employment, something that I was unwilling to accept. In 2016, Wahid Abd Allah Borsh was a thirty-eight-year-old engineer in the UN Development Program. He was arrested by Israeli police in July of that year, suspected of funneling resources to the Hamas terrorist group. The UN response was that as an UN employee, he was entitled to diplomatic immunity. The international body's legal department also demanded that UN officials be granted access to Borsh while he was being held in jail.[59]

In his (and its) defense, the UN cited its Charter, Article 105 specifically, to claim that Borsh, "enjoys immunity from personal arrest or detention, as well as immunity from legal process in respect of words spoken or written and acts done in performance of his mission."[60] Absurd. For me, there was no debate. We can never grant immunity to terrorists. The legal professionals in Jerusalem wanted to discuss the idea, and I decided that we couldn't debate it. I publicly announced that there would be no immunity for terrorists, and in doing so, I set a precedent. I forced the UN to accept my position, which was that the UN's claim that Borsh was an engineer who provided essential services for the organization was false. My position was that Borsh was funneling UN money to projects benefiting Hamas, including a naval base for the terrorist group's military wing.

In light of my allegations, I called on the UN and other organizations to bring additional oversight to how funding is used in the Gaza Strip, and ensure that it reaches the innocent people who need it and not terrorist groups. I told the UN that any dollar spent and any local hire by an international organization must be monitored to ensure they fulfill the purpose of aiding the residents of Gaza and not fund terror activities.[61]

We do not give immunity to anyone suspected of aiding and abetting terrorists. I reject the claim that a person assisting a recognized terrorist organization can hide behind a claim of immunity. In 2016, Borsh did confess to joining the terror group and in 2017 an Israeli court sentenced him to seven months in jail for aiding Hamas in the Gaza Strip.[62]

Never Let Hate Win

November 29, 2017 marked the seventieth anniversary of the partition plan that led to the establishment of the State of Israel. A few months before that date, my staff and I began to plan a reenactment of this historic vote, working together with a few Jewish organizations. The actual event took place in what is today the main gallery of The Queens Museum, in Queens, New York. At the time, this building hosted the UN General Assembly. How festive it would be to mark this momentous accession in this unique way, holding it in the very place where the vote happened.

We spoke to museum officials, including the deputy director, and he agreed to host the reenactment event on the 29th. In fact, there was a great deal of enthusiasm about the event among the museum's staff. The museum personnel we spoke with felt the event would be great visibility for the institution, as it would garner much press attention. This would be important for the museum, given its location, off the conventional Manhattan-based "museum trail" most tourists and New Yorkers are familiar with. Naturally, the museum would receive a rental fee. It would be a win-win for everyone.

Two weeks after we received the initial enthusiastic go-ahead, I received a phone call from then-museum director, Laura Raicovich, informing me that the board had decided not to approve the event after all. I was shocked at this reversal and demanded an explanation. Raicovich told me that the board had reconsidered, now classifying it as a political event, and claiming that "we don't allow political events to take place in the museum."

I was not diplomatic when I discussed the cancellation with Raicovich, who also told me that *anything* concerning Israel would not be allowed at the museum. I rejected the board's decision and the reasoning behind it. This was a historic event, not a political one. The museum director then had the audacity to tell me that we might be able to have the event outside, in late November. My pursuit of answers would not end with this phone call. "I have news for you," I said, "the event will take place inside, but perhaps you will be the one standing outside when it does."

That moment was a personal test for me. For years, I had spoken against the BDS movement, which advocates individuals and institutions stop investing in or buying Israeli products as a way of supporting the Palestinian cause, which it doesn't do. Let me clear up the assumption many may have that Palestinians themselves support the divestment movement; they don't. There are at least fourteen Israeli industrial parks in Judea and Samaria, with nearly 800 manufacturing facilities.[63] These factories employ more than 11,000 Palestinians, paying them two to three times what Palestinians make elsewhere on average. Almost 14 percent of the Palestinian workforce in Judea and Samaria work in Israel. Thousands of Palestinian farmers have worked with Israelis to learn and improve their agricultural techniques.

There are about 130,000 Palestinians who work in Jewish communities, according to the UN Conference on Trade and Development (UNCTAD)[64]—but this number very likely underestimates the actual amount, since many Palestinians cross into Israel to work without permits.[65] Palestinians also benefit from

Israel innovations, technologies, and medicines. There is no reason for Palestinians to support BDS, and every reason in the world to oppose it, which they largely do. Even Palestinian Authority leader Mahmoud Abbas rejects BDS and the boycott of Israel.[66] The only reason to support BDS is to promote hatred.

I have gone to many college campuses to encourage students to speak up and not sit idly by when BDS movements arise. Now I was face to face with a person who is actively engaged in the promotion of BDS. Staying quiet was not an option. I took on the fight and swung into action mode.

If I was going to launch an offense, I had to know what was really behind the decision, and who actually made it. I collected information about the museum, its board of directors, and Raicovich. It didn't take a lot of digging to learn that Raicovich was an active and vocal BDS supporter. She was not an unbiased party. She is co-editor of the book *Assuming Boycott: Resistant, Agency, and Cultural Production*,[67] an anthology that included support of BDS. In the book, she talks specifically about using museums, including the Queens Museum, for political action, including BDS.[68]

I canceled all meetings I had scheduled that day and called every person I knew in the city who could be helpful, including local councilmen, donors to the museum, state politicians, and the mayor's office. Dozens and dozens of calls were made to let people know what was going on and to create a momentum of pressure that would be needed to fight the decision to cancel the event. I had to call many people I didn't know, but I had no problem reaching out to them. All out—that's how you win. You don't say "Maybe I shouldn't." You say, "I should, I can, I must."

Early news reports about the cancellation said pressure from "Palestinian friends" of the museum[69] had proven too much for the board, and it caved. The truth was something quite different. It was an inside job, an autonomous and ideologically-driven action taken by Raicovich herself.

When it became widely known that the museum had reneged on the agreement, it was gratifying to see many people rally in support of the event. Some of my colleagues from Israel thought we might create tension with the mayor's office, because Mayor Bill de Blasio had nominated Laura Raicovich to the position. They were wrong. The senior officials from our Israeli consulate in New York asked to meet me urgently. They were afraid that my campaign would become political against the mayor before his reelection. My answer to them was polite and determined; it was already political and we should not blink or look back. I ignored their calls to be quiet about it. I heard them, and I continued. While the mayor's office kept quiet, many city council members, Jews and non-Jews alike, stood with us publicly. City Council Speaker Melissa Mark-Viverito[70] joined many other lawmakers calling for the museum to reverse its decision.

Not long after, I received a phone call from the chairman of the board of the museum. He wanted to see me, to tell me the museum would indeed have the event inside on the original date. It was the right decision. That day, we also received confirmation that Vice President Mike Pence would participate in the festivities.

I met the chairman of the board, Peter Warwick, in my office the next day, where he apologized to me for what had transpired with the museum director. Before he left the room at the Mission, Warwick told me that the museum board had started an investigation into what happened, and that they had fired the deputy director of the museum, David Strauss. This news made me feel bad, as I knew that Strauss was not the problem. He was a professional and did everything by the book, but the museum wanted a scapegoat. I knew the problem was the director herself but I was not in a position to tell them what to do. From the statement I put out and the interviews I gave in the forty-eight hours before the meeting, they knew exactly what I thought of Raicovich and the book she edited and published.

After a thorough investigation, the museum did determine Raicovich to be at fault. The report,[71] which was made public, found that Raicovich "showed immediate hostility to hosting the event at the museum even before consulting with the board." The three-month investigation reviewed more than six thousand emails and conducted twenty-plus interviews. It concluded that Raicovich "knowingly misled" the board and "failed to comport... with the standards consistent with [her position]." It also revealed that Raicovich told the board that the museum had a policy prohibiting political events when no such policy existed. In other words, she lied to me and to her own board of directors.

Even if such a policy existed, the event was not political but a reenactment of an actual historical event that had taken place in the very hall of the museum. This fight was covered by the press both in New York and internationally. That we prevailed sent a strong message to thousands of Jewish students and others who have to confront BDS daily that you can win when you have conviction, courage, and persistence.

On the day of the event, we were concerned that there would be BDS protesters outside the venue to try and spoil the day, but there was nothing like that. It was a mega event with hundreds of UN representatives, ambassadors, and other officials in attendance who were able to enjoy and learn from the reenactment in peace. When one fellow ambassador asked me why Vice President Pence was attending, it made me realize what the event really meant, how powerful it was. It was remarkable that he came. When Vice President Pence spoke, he hinted at moving the US embassy to Jerusalem. The event was meaningful from a historical perspective, and it also showed the strong bond between the US and Israel that continues to exist today. Laura Raicovich "resigned" a few months after the event, but it is more likely she was removed.

False Claims Must be Countered

There were other such battles at the UN. In the early 2000s and even before, many of our radical adversaries were pushing the idea of comparing Israel to the South African apartheid regime. Our enemies used this language to try to apply the same sanctions against us that were used against South Africa, for the cause of the Palestinians. It is an effort to label Israel as an apartheid state, which is not the case in any way, shape, or form. It's a complete mischaracterization and a dangerous one. I call the use of this kind of language diplomatic terrorism. It also includes passing anti-Israel resolutions.

The goal behind this diplomatic terrorism campaign is to create an environment or mechanism that will force an agreement without negotiations between us and Palestinians. Unfortunately, the Palestinian leadership doesn't want to negotiate. They are only interested in bashing us day and night. I am convinced that their leadership is focused on promoting hate against Israel rather than promoting their own interests. They truly believe that the hate and incitement will force us to accept a bad agreement. This strategy never works. However, they envision portraying us as an apartheid state or as a rogue regime to put us in a precarious position with the international community. It has not worked in the past and it will not work in the future.

There are many UN agencies and groups. One way to create more pressure on Israel and ostensibly support the Palestinian "cause" is by passing resolutions that require a yearly report about Israel, which are always highly critical. We deal with dozens of such reports every year. One report in particular, which was written and issued in March 2017, during my tenure at the UN, once again used the language of apartheid to condemn Israel. The report, "Israeli Practices Toward the Palestinian People and the Question of Apartheid,"[72] was published by the UN Economic and Social Commission for Western Asia (ESCWA). The ESCWA, headquartered in Beirut, has eighteen Arab state members, two of which, at this point—Jordan and Egypt—had peace treaties with Israel. However, the report was actually written by American Richard Falk, a former UN special rapporteur to the Palestinian territories known for his harsh criticisms of Israel and the United States, and Virginia Tilley, professor of political science at Southern Illinois University.

The two authors concluded that Israel had established an apartheid regime aimed at dominating the Palestinians. Their recommendations include reviving the UN Center Against Apartheid, which closed in 1994 after South Africa ended its apartheid practices. The report also urged support for a BDS campaign against Israel.

A public statement following up on the report was released by Rima Khalaf, a UN undersecretary general and executive secretary of ESCWA. It reiterated her absurd claim that Israel had established an apartheid regime, and it was "not an easy matter for a United Nations entity."

The approach I took on this and other outrageous reports was zero tolerance. The committee that issued this report was not part of the security council, but Khalaf took advantage of her position to promote ideas against Israel. When things like this happen, you have three choices. The first is to ignore it and hope no one pays attention to it, and that happened on many occasions with my predecessors. Some Israeli diplomats would say, let it go and ignore it. The second option is to present a diplomatic statement clarifying your objections to the content of the report. This could be in the form of a formal letter to the secretary general for the record. This was a common response from the Israeli mission before I arrived.

The third way, which I continue to promote, was to fight back, and not to ignore such reports or just write formal complaint letters about them. The professional team at the mission told me it was not the first time or the last time such reports would be issued, and not to make a scene. I did not accept that recommendation. Even if we cannot change anything, the people writing the reports, issuing them, and presenting them at the UN need to understand that we are paying attention and reading every word in every report. We need to challenge the reports and call them out in public. We would absolutely make a scene.

My approach was risky, and I was fully aware of this. If I make a public issue of it and it fails, it's not pleasant. However, my attitude is that it is a win-win even if I fail, because my response makes it clear that we will not sit by and allow these reports to go unnoticed and unchallenged. People will understand that when they report in this way, they have to answer for it. It's always worth it in situations like this.

I began to lobby against Khalaf. I met with Ambassador Nikki Haley and other ambassadors to discuss next steps. Nikki told me she would take action against the report on the spot, unlike other ambassadors who told me they would have to check with their capitals before taking immediate action. I also met with the secretary general, António Guterres, who needed to understand that when he signs these reports, even though he signs dozens of them over the course of the year, and has no time to actually read them, the people of Israel and the world believe that in signing the report he has endorsed it. The secretary general was very sincere with me. He said, "Danny, I was not aware of it, I have not read it."

A few things happened after that meeting. First, the report was withdrawn from the UN website. UN Secretary General Guterres distanced himself from the findings, with spokesman Stéphane Dujarric saying the report was published without any prior consultation with the UN secretariat. "The report as it stands does not reflect the views of the secretary general," said Dujarric.

I met with other ambassadors, made many phone calls, and was assured that the UN Secretary General would receive many calls from ambassadors, leaders in the Jewish community, and other prominent friends of Israel to express their displeasure at the report and put pressure on him to distance himself from it and delegitimize it. This adds up when the calls and pressure reach a certain point. I was relieved and felt satisfied when the statement came that Khalaf would resign. Everyone at every UN mission knew exactly why. It was not because of other issues but only because of the report against Israel. Khalaf resigned from her position. The fact that we applied pressure and she resigned was a strong achievement, and it sent a message to other bureaucrats at the UN that we were watching for and reading every word against us. We would take notes and bring up and respond to any falsehoods.

It is more than worthwhile to enter the struggles and fight. The lesson I learned, when it comes to confronting enemies of Israel, is that even when we do not know what the outcome will be, it is worth the fight.

Another positive outcome from speaking out about this report was that the secretary general instituted a new procedure in his office, which basically required every report signed by the secretary general's office to be approved by him personally. For us, this was a great outcome, because UN bureaucrats will now think twice about the language they use in reports. The secretary general's chief of staff complained about the work I brought to the office, but they hired someone to take care of examining the reports and to make amendments before they are published.

The message is that Israel cannot ignore falsehoods, especially those entered into public forums. This is an ongoing fight in which we must participate. We have no problem with criticism or unpleasant facts. We want to engage in dialogue. It is the political agenda we have a problem with, and it is a problem we should not and will not ignore.

CHAPTER EIGHT

Israel Must Accentuate Its Benefits

*Defending against criticism is justified, but we
must show the solutions we bring to the table.*

I cannot emphasize enough the importance of building bridges
and furthering your cause through friendly relationships and
partnerships, collaboration, and sharing information, knowledge,
and experience. Instead of focusing on conflicts and problems,
one should bring new and positive agenda items to the table, especially in forums like the UN that are accustomed to putting a great
deal of energy into criticizing Israel. Those initiatives are fundamental in softening hostilities and changing opinions. Doing so is
also part of my obligation, as it is for all Jews, to practice *tikkun
olam*, a concept in Judaism that calls for us to behave and act con-
structively and beneficially to help repair the world.

Part of the homework I gave myself when I began my ambassadorship was to identify what I could do to put Israel in the best
light, by sharing with other ambassadors and countries those technologies, innovations, and information that I know would help
their economies and social fabric improve. Before every meeting with a colleague, I would prepare a list of topics Israel could
offer to help them with. Instead of speaking about problems, I

spoke about solutions. Instead of speaking about our differences, I focused on what we have in common.

When one thinks about the work of the ambassadors at the UN, there is the tendency to think only about the interaction between member states in the different bodies of the general assembly and the security council, various committees, and between countries. Actually, a major part of the work of every mission is to work with the UN secretary's office and its officials. When you look at the famous building on the East River of Manhattan, you must understand it holds hundreds of offices with thousands of employees of all kinds. There is a great deal of interaction between each member state and the UN. For Israel, it used to be a relationship based on debates and arguments, where we were trying to push back against any involvement of UN organs in our area. Today, there is a different reality. We understand the potential of cooperation, especially the ability to share our technology with the UN itself, and to increase our involvement on "soft" issues, which will improve Israel's global standing.

There are two dimensions in how Israel works with the UN. The first is Israel working with the UN itself and its internal or organizational departments. The second dimension is the bilateral relations between countries, or country to country, ambassador to ambassador. The personal relationship between ambassadors is a key component of diplomacy. Although we have embassies in different countries, you can accomplish things much faster working through the UN. Most ambassadors have a direct line to their head of state, and you can get answers on the spot.

Many times, when a world leader wanted to visit Israel, I would receive a call from a colleague from the country in question for help in arranging and finalizing the visit. I would then call the prime minister, who was always happy to host heads of states. Hence, I received a green light to approve the visits. It took me a while to realize that our ministry of foreign affairs had limited manpower to coordinate those visits, which is why they were always pushing people off to visit the following year. I thought this was a mistake, and I convinced the prime minister to give clear instructions that we would be honored to host any head of state whenever they requested to come.

After coordinating a few visits, the Israeli director general of the ministry of foreign affairs called to tell me that he felt I was bypassing our embassies in different countries in facilitating these official requests. I replied that the fact that an ambassador approached me in New York was because they never received a reply from anyone else. They knew I would get back to them.

A Bounty of Good

We have so much to offer as a young, start-up nation. Israelis have constructed a powerhouse economy in the middle of the Levant, a place where there are few natural resources. Over the last few decades, we have made incredible economic, social, and technological advancements. Cut diamonds, high-technology equipment, and pharmaceuticals are among our leading exports,[73] along with human capital—researchers, scholars, scientists, innovators, and entrepreneurs—which has brought great abundance to our own economy and to the world. Science and technology are two of our most developed sectors. We spend almost 5 percent of our gross domestic product[74] (GDP) on civil research and development, the highest ratio in the world. In 2019, Israel was ranked by Bloomberg[75] as the world's fifth most innovative country. It also has one of the highest per capita rates of filed patents[76].

When you look at where we are today compared to our neighbors, our success in a short period of time is even more remarkable. The average Israeli income is about twice the average of our neighbors. In fact, Israel's GDP per person is about ten times that of our neighbors, due in great part to our amazing economic growth in just the last thirty years. Since 1985 to today, the Israeli economy grew by a factor of ten,[77] as it expanded from agriculture to biotechnology,[78] aviation, pharmaceuticals, and communications products.

Israel also scores high in terms of economic freedom, 73.8, making its economy the twenty-sixth freest in the 2021 Heritage Foundation Index.[79] Israel is ranked second among fourteen countries in the Middle East and North Africa, and its overall score is above both regional and world averages.

We work hard to continue to maintain our spirit of innovation. I've been asked many times how we achieved this. There are a few facts worth mentioning. First, we had no other option. We either had to resign ourselves to a constant struggle, or we had to resolve to think out of the box to overcome our natural environment and build an advanced society from the ground up. We could not allow ourselves to be lazy; this would be both dangerous and ineffective. We wanted to thrive, and we chose to do so. We thought about solutions and ideas. If we had been in an oil-rich part of the region, we may not have developed this spirit. In many ways, then, we are fortunate not to live in a place that provides oil.

The second factor is that immigration from the Soviet Union, which included many educated people, engineers, technicians, teachers, scientists, and researchers, brought an infusion of knowledge to Israel. More than one million people immigrated, and most were educated. This was not the only factor, but it is an instrumental one. Everyone agrees about the importance of this wave of immigration. We would be less secure today without this influx of people who strengthened our economy.

A third factor is that we have a mandatory military service for young men and women. It allows them to assume leadership positions at an early age and gain valuable experience. At twenty-one, they are already mature and experienced, because everyone capable who graduates from high school at eighteen must go into mandatory military service. The roles are quite varied and suit each person's talents. Some study and practice cybersecurity, others learn computer programming or maintenance, while others do field work. The on-the-ground experience of taking a leadership role and learning responsibility gives us tremendous currency nationally, regionally, and globally.

We also give these young minds the freedom to come up with new ideas and try them out. This not only helps our military, but it also enables the private sector and our economy to expand. Young people completing their service and leaving the military have developed the confidence to start their own companies, develop their own ideas, or bring them to established companies. This happens time and again, because we offer so much support for innovators and innovation. This is essential for any society or nation to remain strong, secure, and on the forefront of ideas that can and do change the world.

I would like to mention a few examples of Israeli innovation that I exposed in different events at the UN.

The firewall, the original protection against malware, is software that protects our data from dangerous criminal cyber activity. It is one of the cornerstones of computer security and perhaps the greatest computer technology invention from Israel. Gil Shwed, Marius Nacht, and Shlomo Kramer of Israel-based Check Point Software Technologies developed the first viable commercial firewall in 1993.

Netafim is a desert-friendly irrigation system that has enabled Israeli farmers who previously struggled to grow crops in our arid climate. Its technology ensures that food crops receive proper irrigation. In 1965, engineer Simcha Blass observed two adjacent trees, one small, the other larger. A water pipe sat next to the large tree, and he saw that it had a small crack, allowing water to slowly drip out of it. This was a lightbulb moment for Blass, who understood that slow but regular drips of water were enough to allow for vigorous plant growth. This led to his development of a micro-irrigation system, which made it possible to grow crops using a limited amount of water. By 1967, Netafim's invention had improved crop yields by 70 percent in the Arava desert in Israel, while simultaneously reducing water usage in the region. Today, Netafim is used in 110 countries and has helped restore almost twenty-five million acres of land.

Watergen produces quality drinking water from air. You heard that right. The air. Watergen, started in 2010, uses a system that extracts humidity from the air in places as diverse as rainforests to desert climates like Israel's. The technology also uses filtration technology to eliminate pollutants found in the air, purifying it, and making it safe for human consumption. The device has been used in disaster zones across the globe, including 2017's Hurricane Maria in Puerto Rico.

Scientist Gavriel Iddan of Given Imaging (now Medtronic) invented the PillCam, a digestible, disposable camera that transmits data to a receiver outside the body. FDA-approved, the PillCam is now used all over the world to diagnose infection, intestinal disorders, and cancers in the digestive system. It can also access areas of the digestive system that are typically out of range during a conventional procedure. Iddan received the European Inventor Award in 2011, fourteen years after the prototype was first released.

This is a small sampling of the kinds of ideas and innovations that come from Israel. The public education systems in other countries, such as Singapore and Poland, might be better than ours, or perhaps more rigorous. But when you look at our spirit of innovation and industriousness, we are unsurpassed. Few can compete with it unless they are willing to change their attitudes. It is our openness, enthusiasm, and support that encourages people to come up with new ideas and pursue them. Israel must continue to invest in technical and scientific education to ensure we have enough people developing technologies and medicine; we must also continue to be an attractive home for any Jew who wants to relocate to their homeland.

In 2015, during my service as minister of science and technology, a delegation of Chinese business investors came to see me. I asked the Chinese delegation to be specific about the investments they were interested in, and if they had any specific fields they wanted to invest in in Israel: health, biotechnology, or agriculture. Their answer was shocking. They told me that if it was Jewish, they wanted to invest in it, having the idea that anything we produced had to be superior in quality. I found this slightly amusing but also quite fascinating because the delegation's enthusiasm reinforced the idea that we are admired and recognized globally as a technology and innovation powerhouse. My knowledge of the field would help me. I conducted a deep dive into the latest innovations from Israel that could have applications around the globe. I would leverage this recognition with both developed and developing countries at the UN as I sought to promote Israeli businesses, build bridges, and open the UN itself to using Israeli-made products.

I realized we could offer numerous valuable technologies and other commodities to the UN, which is very similar to a large corporation. We looked at the UN itself as a large market and wanted to embrace it for potential mutual benefits. The UN has 37,000 employees across 193 international offices. In Manhattan alone, there are 5,000 employees. As a large organization, it has a significant budget and a robust procurement department.

I obviously understood that the UN had an ingrained hostility toward Israel. It would be an uphill battle to form a working relationship with its procurement department. When I first approached the idea of procurement with the UN, the administrative personnel, as I predicted, were hesitant to do business with us because of this historically hostile environment. This was despite the fact that they purchase goods and services from countries around the world, including medical supplies from the United States, helicopters from Russia, and so on.

We also made meaningful headway in terms of Israelis working in visible positions at the UN. While there are Israelis who work in security positions at the organization, there are not many Israeli employees at the UN in general. I wanted to change that. I identified an opportunity to promote a skilled and experienced Israeli terrorism expert who was already working on the UN committee, but not in a senior position. I felt he was the right candidate to earn a promotion. I discussed this idea with his superior, and while he agreed that this man, Dudi Zechia, was the best candidate, because he was Israeli it would be a challenge to promote him. There would be pushback against his nomination. This is a problem with the UN—many experienced, highly skilled, and knowledgeable Israelis are blocked because of where they come from.

I didn't let this challenge stop me. Dudi was the best candidate and deserved the promotion. If he won it, it would mean Israel would have someone in a senior position at the UN for the first time. As expected, once his name was brought in front of the committee, we received an immediate rejection from some of the Arab countries. I was disappointed; even Egypt, with whom we have close ties, issued a public letter against the nomination. Usually when that happens, the nomination stops and goes no further. Not this time. I was determined not to give up, and I continued to lobby on Dudi's behalf.

During a visit of the UN Secretary General Ban-ki Moon with Israel, there were two meetings with the prime minister. One was with advisors and senior staff, and the other was between Ban-ki Moon and the prime minister. Our ministry of foreign affairs had prepared a list of fifteen issues to be discussed between the two men. This was too many topics; they would never get through such a list. I narrowed it down to three subjects, two were terrorism related, and one was the nomination of Dudi to this important position. The prime minister asked me about it, and I explained to him that this nomination was a test case for us, and that we could no longer allow our adversaries to block Israelis from holding senior positions at the UN.

I was not sure if he would bring it up. The minute the secretary general walked out of the meeting, he called his senior under-secretary for political affairs, Jeffrey Feltman, an American diplomat, and told him that he wanted him to immediately deal with the issue of Dudi's hire. I happened to overhear this exchange as I was in the room. The promotion went through. It was a great victory, and Dudi has served in the position with excellence. But it took the involvement of both the prime minister and the secretary general to make it happen.

Essentially, in the past the UN was unofficially practicing BDS, because they were avoiding purchasing or engagement with Israeli companies. When we talk about BDS, it's not always done publicly or even with full consciousness. Many times, toxic BDS propaganda campaigns create a chilling effect; some will not even think about it but will try to avoid conflicts and will quietly boycott Israel. That was the case with the UN. There was no guideline advocating for an Israeli boycott, but that was the reality. Again, I was told it's a lost cause, that I shouldn't even try to get the UN to buy from Israel. The feeling was it would be a useless attempt because the UN would cave to pressure and pushback from some in the Arab world, as well as from some Western countries who had their own economic interests.

I believed in our ability to change the situation because I knew the quality, value, and function of what we had to offer would overcome any hesitancy over political or ideological concerns. Strategically, it was important that we at least try. When I arrived at the UN, I made a more concerted push to do business with the UN. The engagement would be good for us in so many ways. I always stress that we must not speak only of politics and conflict during security council debates. We need to expose all that we have to offer in technology, capabilities, knowledge, and innovation. It's important from an economic aspect to help Israeli companies sell their products, but it is also vital for national security. I knew once the UN worked with Israeli companies, Israeli technology would be appreciated, and it would help shift opinions about us.

Motivation and persistence would be necessary to make it happen, and I had both. My vision included the three stages, which I called the Three Ts. We would sell our relevant technology, offer training, and provide troops. The first two would turn out to be much easier to implement than the last. In fact, during my tenure, we did accomplish the first two. We now share our enormous knowledge about disasters and recovery in the form of training. In terms of the medical field, the UN uses Israeli training experts to teach its trainers around the world in medical procedures of all kinds, especially when it comes to treating serious casualties in the field and setting up field hospitals. We are experts in these areas out of necessity. There is much appreciation for our experts in this practice area.

Doing Business for Good

As for sharing technology at and through the UN, it was challenging but doable. Indeed, Israel has long been a leader in unmanned aerial vehicles or UAV technology, produced beginning in the late 1970s to counter threats on the Egyptian and Syrian frontlines. Later we successfully used the technology to produce surveillance imagery during the 1982 battles against Syrian air defenses. More global players entered the field, and now there are an array of countries producing sophisticated systems, including the US, China, and even Turkey.[80]

This is to say that while today there is a great deal of competition in the drone market, it's also a big playing field with huge demand. Israel has a few niches in drone technology. Israeli manufacturers continue to produce smaller drones and high-altitude surveillance UAVs, but we are also pioneering counter-UAV technology. Our Iron Dome missile defense system can be used against drones. Some makers have experimented with laser systems that shoot down enemy drones. We're also building small loitering munitions, sometimes referred to as "kamikaze drones." They are essentially flying warheads that can return to base if they are not deployed. However, their purpose is to hover over a target, wait for an enemy to appear in range, and deploy a perfectly timed precision strike.[81] The point is, we have specialized technology and often build from necessity, but these can be used by others for their own defense and security needs.

Right now, our drones are used mainly for military purposes, but they can also be used for peacekeeping operations. When I met with a UN senior official who was in charge of procurement—a very powerful job—he told me that while he valued our friendship and relationship, and appreciated our innovation capabilities, he could not buy anything from Israel because he was afraid of the pushback he would get from Arab countries. Regarding this bid, the official told me there were a few companies they were considering. He told me he would likely choose a European company. He felt if he chose an Israeli firm, it would create a lot of problems. Even though it was just another line in the budget, there might be people who would notice and make an issue of it, and not just in the halls of the UN between ambassadors. It could become a topic of debate in UN forums and perhaps in the press. I was skeptical this would be the case, and so what if it was true? It would be forgotten soon enough, and I knew our products were superior.

I asked to see a model of the European drone under consideration. I looked at it and told him if that was what he wanted to buy, he should know that both its engine and camera were developed and manufactured in Israel. These two parts are the heart and soul of a drone's function. I looked him straight in the eye and said, "You are not buying a European drone, but an expensive Israeli drone." In other words, buying a similar if not better drone directly from Israel would save the UN a great deal of money—and give them a better product.

He was convinced by my strong words and promised to give it a try. The UN is naturally always worried about the well-being of its troops in conflict areas. When we offer solutions that protect those troops, it can mean the difference between life and death, and that's important. I identified two Israeli companies who make the drone, and they put in a bid. For me, it was important that the drones come from an Israeli company; I didn't care which one. The undersecretary promised that he would pick the best product without a political shadow over the decisions. One of the Israeli companies actually won the bid. That was a great opening.

These manufacturers also provide services along with the purchase. They send people to teach the UN how to use the equipment and offer training to whoever it deems necessary. In that sense, these companies are not just selling a drone and walking away. They are selling a great deal of knowledge, technological support, and follow-up education. The UN was happy with the technology and services. This first entry into the UN procurement system allowed us to enter many other bids for technology and devices that helped protect the UN peacekeeping missions. He gave us a chance, and since then, we have continued to sell drones to the UN. We sold other products, too, including identification technologies that help control people coming in and out of UN bases at their gates. Ultimately, the undersecretary was worried for no reason, because as I had predicted, there was no outcry about the UN drone purchase. No one cared. I proved that you can successfully help people understand what Israeli technologies can bring to the world.

When the pope visited Africa, the UN purchased an Israeli surveillance balloon made by Israeli company RT Aerostats Systems to ensure His Holiness traveled safely. These balloons have cameras that can see in a thirty-mile circumference to see if any threats are coming near. If so, the system alerts security forces in a balloon control room. The manufacturer offers training so that anyone, anywhere, using the technology can see what is happening around a potential target, whether they are in a jungle, a desert, or a heavily populated urban area.

The balloon proved more reliable than unmanned air vehicles, which are typically to protect dignitaries in similar circumstances, and the balloons cost a fraction of the price to operate, compared to conventional technologies. The balloon device was also used at two of the three Masses led by the pope when he was in Colombia. An RT Aerostats official told reporters that, "In addition to advanced day and night cameras, the balloon can automatically identify suspicious movements, better zoom in on targets we want to follow, and maintain an overview of the entire area even while focusing on a specific target." Police in Bogota and Medellin leased the device and transmitted its video footage directly to their headquarters. It helped scan large crowds, rooftops, and other spots that cannot be seen from the ground.[82]

I was proud of making headway with the first two Ts at the UN: training and technology. Those are the areas I focused on first, because it was the right thing to do to reach out and work with the UN in as many ways as we could. Countries are also more willing to work with us in these two areas.

I believe the last T, providing troops to UN peacekeeping missions, will come in time. Sending troops is still an ongoing effort on our part. We have one of the best-trained militaries in the world, and it knows how to deal with many difficult conflicts. We have so many security challenges that require us to engage in prevention, deflection, and defense that it puts us in a unique position of having both the know-how and the experience on the ground. This gives us an advantage in comparison to others. We have the expertise to train UN forces, such as search and rescue, medical treatment in the field, and addressing acute emergency situations.

I was able to start a dialogue about it. I believe the best way to make inroads in this area is not by sending Israeli soldiers to peacekeeping missions, but instead, offering the help of Israeli police forces. These men and women are highly trained, and I know they could be incredibly useful in helping the UN. It has not happened yet, but I am hopeful. It remains a goal for the future.

We have made headway with our police force. For instance, we sent some of our highly trained officers to Haiti after devastating earthquakes not just to help, but to teach their law enforcement people how to maintain law and order. We know how to mobilize quickly and will gladly share our techniques for doing so. Even though we are not able to send troops to UN peacekeeping missions—yet—we *can* send fast-response crews to affected areas during a crisis very quickly. When the building collapse happened in Surfside, Florida in June 2021, Israel not only sent drones and search and rescue teams, but we also sent reserve soldiers who are highly skilled and trained in disaster recovery.[83] They were there within a few hours of being called.

We also want to do the right thing whenever and wherever possible that use our strengths in ways aside from security, defense, and disaster relief. For example, we have a project in Israel called Save a Child's Heart (SACH). This international non-profit organization's central mission is to improve the quality of pediatric cardiac care for children from developing countries who suffer from heart disease and who cannot get adequate medical care in their homelands. Children with rheumatic and congenital heart disease around the world often suffer because they have no access to care or the medical knowledge and training to treat their conditions. SACH brings children to Israel for treatment, and it also trains doctors in other countries in life-saving medicine and surgeries. When we can do this for children in Africa and other developing nations, it shifts the conversation away from negative stereotypes about Israel to the positives we bring to the table. The organization (and others like it) have also saved the lives of thousands of Palestinian children.[84] I was very proud when Save a Child's Heart received the UN's Population Award in 2018, the first time the global body officially recognized an Israeli NGO with an award.[85]

It's important to note that the absurdity of BDS is thrown into high relief when people realize how much everyone in the world benefits from Israel's innovations and manufacturing. But people only know this if you tell them. As I mentioned earlier, one of the first things I did after my appointment to the UN was to initiate a project that would bring ambassadors to Israel and show them some of the technological advancements Israel makes and shares with the world—specific things we can help their countries with. Drip irrigation system, cell phone components, drones, life-saving medical masks, important pharmaceuticals, and many other products come from Israel. If you really want to boycott Israeli innovation, do so at your own peril. When you understand a people, work with them, get exposed to them, and see how they contribute to the world and community, you are less threatened by them.

In many African countries, sourcing clean water is a problem. I hosted a dinner at the house of a respected Jewish family for some of the African ambassadors and brought in Israeli experts on water sourcing, purification, and delivery. These scientists and developers discussed many solutions that were both affordable and effective. The ambassadors were both amazed and excited. They wanted to stay for hours after the event ended to continue the discussion of these technologies with the engineers and others I had brought in. For these ambassadors, the information shared at the event was a revelation. They hear the claim that Israel is the source of all the world's problems rather than the source of many of its solutions. This event went a long way in showing that Israel is a part of the solution to serious challenges.

Countries that deal with crucial issues of water and food security every day see finding solutions as a priority that we can help them with. With all due respect to issues in the Middle East, ambassadors from developing nations care much more about solving problems in their own countries and for their own people. Solving problems that are not of their making, and in places thousands of miles away, are just not a priority. They understand the futility of this. Israel can be a partner in helping, but we must stay modest about it. After all, we are a small country, and Africa is a huge continent with many people. While we cannot solve all their problems, we can come up with good ideas and workable technology for some of them.

We have had to deal with major terror attacks in the past. As a result, we have developed the knowledge and know-how to respond to massive disasters and search and rescue missions. Today, we offer not only training, but we also deploy our units to help whenever there is a natural disaster. We have the ability to quickly mobilize emergency assistance, and we have done so in Haiti, Nepal, and many other locations. Within hours, we can have a field hospital set up with doctors and nurses working on the ground. This is what we did when Mexico had a major earthquake in September 2017, coincidently during a high-level week for the UN General Assembly.[86] I was hosting Prime Minister Netanyahu on his annual visit to the UN. After we learned about the earthquake, we tried to contact Mexico, but lines were down and there was no communication.

I was friendly with the Mexican ambassador to the UN, Juan Jose Gomez Camacho. Prime Minister Netanyahu was heading back to Israel before the holiday. He gave me the green light to reach out to Ambassador Camacho and offer our help in the search and rescue mission. I was able to talk to the ambassador, and he was happy with the offer of help. He suggested we connect the minister of foreign affairs, Luis Videgaray Caso, to the prime minister. I told him I'd do so quickly to finalize the details around the help we wanted to send.

At the time, I was on my way to JFK airport as part of the prime minister's convoy of twenty cars and SWAT teams escorting us. I was one car behind the prime minister. There is generally a small ceremony when we greet each other at the plane as the prime minister is about to board. Once we arrived at the airport, I asked the prime minister to stay in his car so he could speak to the Mexican foreign minister. Prime Minister Netanyahu did so and offered support. After the call ended, I spoke with the Mexican ambassador to follow up on all the details. The prime minister's plane had left, and instructions to mobilize a field hospital with a search and rescue unit to Mexico City were delivered to Jerusalem.

Once we activated the search and rescue unit, it took the team a matter of hours to get in the air to Mexico City. The reason it happened so fast was because we always have field hospital equipment at the ready in an airport hangar. The unit, which is made up of medical teams, keep their medical "go bags" packed and ready to go in their homes. As soon as they receive a text message they are needed, it takes them a short time to prepare and get to the airport. These reservists put everything behind them during these times and go where they are needed. Such was the case when they were called to fly to Mexico City. Because there were no delays, we were the first one on the ground helping them look for survivors using our expertise in search and rescue. Once the team completed the mission, they were cheered on in the streets of Mexico City for their help.[87] It was an emotional moment. Of course, when the US arrives to a catastrophic event, it's a massive response, and there is no comparison. However, the fact that Israel can respond so quickly allows us to give help immediately until needed reinforcements arrive.

Although we've made a great deal of headway convincing the UN itself to use what we had to offer, as well as convincing countries who may be influenced by our enemies that we can help them, the job of convincing them of our sincerity is not over. It will always be a challenge; you always have political pressure. Promoting Israeli products will always be a hard sell at the UN.

That's why I launched a special seminar in New York aimed at fostering increased business ties between Israeli companies and the UN. We focused on furthering existing cooperation and building new business relationships between the UN and the Israeli private sector. During the two-day event, companies from the security, cyber, information communications technology (ICT), environment, water and sanitation industries met with the various UN departments and agencies that spend $17 billion annually on goods and services from around the world. We made a great deal of headway in terms of showing the benefits of Israeli-made products and creating partnerships for Israeli businesses with the UN.

In order to continue to persuade, we have to be present and proactive. I was elected to chair the UN Science and Technology Innovation Forum (STI) in the beginning of 2020. Two ambassadors chair the forum, and I was joined by the ambassador of Ghana, Martha Ama Akyaa Pobee, a good friend of mine who came with me on a mission to Israel and was always open to collaboration. I was excited that both of us would be chairing the forum together. We have so much knowledge, so chairing the committee with a developing country creates amazing opportunities.

Shortly after, we began to plan and organize a two-day technology event. We intended to focus on the connection between developed and developing countries. Our aim was to show new and advanced technologies from developed countries that could help the developing world. Then UN ambassador from Norway, Mona Juul, who chaired the Economic Social Council, called me to what she said was an urgent meeting. She told me how much she cared about Israel, but that she was getting heat from the Organization of Islamic Countries (OIC) because I was elected to chair the forum.

The OIC knew how influential I had become at the UN. It was my fifth year there, and I had built a reputation of someone who gets things done and does not back down. Our adversaries knew that I would make sure the event was meaningful. It would attract positive publicity. Many of the technologies on display would be the result of Israel's know-how and innovation. This was untenable for the OIC and its supporters. That is why they opposed it. Those individuals complaining about our presence on the committee were worried about the positive attention Israel would receive. I pushed back, pointing out that when I was elected to the legal committee, everyone accepted it and life went on. Besides, to object to an event because Israel might get positive press for lending a hand to developing nations was absurd.

The real reason for Juul's concern was that Norway, her home country, was running for the security council in a few months. Its competitors were Ireland and Canada. There were only two open seats. Juul was afraid my presence on the committee would upset the Arab League and eventually lead to Norway losing votes in what would become a tight race. I told her that she should not allow others to blackmail her and not to be intimidated by them. I told her that this technique of intimidation and threats of withholding votes was also used by the Arab League against the ambassador of Canada. You know it is a lie because two candidates have to be chosen out of three, they can't blackmail both Norway and Canada. They were bluffing. It was time to call their bluff. We agreed to continue our discussion.

Not long after this exchange, Martha's husband passed away unexpectedly, and she immediately flew back home to Ghana. I received a phone call from Ambassador Juul shortly after this. On that call, she informed me that Martha had decided not to stay on the technology committee. Because of that, both of our nominations, hers and mine, would be canceled.

It was a way out for the Norwegian ambassador. She tried to use Martha's unfortunate loss as an excuse to cancel our nominations. I told her I wanted to look into it, and I would speak with Martha myself. After conveying my deep condolences about the tragic loss of her husband, we discussed the forum. Martha told me that she did not volunteer to resign, and it was not her intention to do so. I assured her that I would take on most of the preparation necessary so she could remain in Ghana for a while. When she returned, we would chair the forum together. She was very happy to hear this, and we continued to proceed. I looked forward to leading the forum with Martha. I thought, now nothing could block us from moving forward with the event.

I started to prepare the content for the conference with my team and the deputy from the mission of Ghana. We had a schedule of panels mapped out and were happy with the result. Once we completed the itinerary, we assembled the list of guests and prepared invitations. This was in early 2020. Now, Ambassador Juul had found another reason to stop the session, and this one was semi-legitimate: COVID-19. We didn't give up. We demanded that this event, like other major events at the UN, would proceed virtually. She did not agree, but we overcame that obstacle too. Martha and I were determined to make a meaningful event. We partnered with Japan and Mexico and demanded to continue the forum in a virtual format. At this point, Juul could not deny us the opportunity to go forward. Everything was set, and the participants were eager to present and attend virtually.

Ultimately, the event was successful both in terms of participants and publicity. It was especially important given that we were in the midst of a pandemic. We showed the connectivity between nations and dug deeply into the ways technologically advanced countries could lend a hand to developing countries, especially during times of crisis and emergency.

In my opening remarks, I made it a point to thank Ambassador Juul for "all" of her assistance in getting the conference off the ground and helping to make it such a success. This is precisely what she didn't want me to do, but how could I not make sure everyone knew how "instrumental" she was to this event?

Martha had also demonstrated her loyalty and friendship in this case. I was very happy to congratulate her when she was elected as Assistant Secretary-General of the United Nations for Africa.

It's vital to continue to push to participate at every level when it comes to sharing our assets with the world, even though it means continually fighting for a place at the table. Technology is here to stay, Israel is here to stay, and our capabilities at innovation are not going anywhere. I believe we can do more as a country in terms of sharing knowledge and helping others. We can and we should. When people realize what we have to offer, it becomes very clear that remaining hostile to the home of world-class scientists, researchers, and innovators is a fool's journey. The more people around the world who value Israel's skills and talents, the stronger and safer we become.

CHAPTER NINE

Run the Marathon

There are intractable problems that we
must commit to fight; we cannot allow
frustration to bring paralysis.

In recent years, a renewed wave of antisemitism has swept across the globe and has eroded the sense of security of Jewish populations[88] everywhere. In many countries, this has been demonstrated through violent attacks on Jewish individuals and groups,[89],[90] synagogues,[91],[92] and neighborhoods and businesses.[93]

It's nothing new, unfortunately. Walter Reich, Senior Scholar at the Woodrow Wilson Center and former director of the United States Holocaust Memorial Museum, explains that antisemitism is the oldest form of bigotry; it's been going on for two millennia.[94] This raises the question: What can be done to reduce and combat antisemitism?

We live in what some people call the "age of wokeness" that has brought about a heightened awareness and sensitivity to ethnically and racially-based bigotry. That's significant, but while certain kinds of hate crimes make headlines, including violence against other minorities, and more recently on the Asian community, an unfortunate result of the COVID pandemic, crimes against Jews continue to take the lead in hate crimes. It's not a competition we want to win. The FBI reports that antisemitism remains the number one hate crime in the US. The Bureaus' data shows Jewish people and institutions were most frequently targeted, accounting for 58 percent of religious-based hate crime incidents. Antisemitism in the United States rose by 80 percent. In the UK, the number of anti-Semitic incidents increased by 570 percent.

Before COVID, Muslims were the second most frequent target, at 18.6 percent, less than a third of the number of anti-Semitic attacks. In 2020, hate crimes against Asian-descent people rose in the US to the number two spot but were still far outweighed by attacks against Jews.[95] The FBI has been keeping records on hate crimes since 1996, and it shows that while hate crimes against blacks have declined by more than a third, the number of anti-Semitic crimes, measured proportionate to the population, hasn't declined or even changed that much.[96] In many other countries, especially in Europe, attacks against Jews have increased.[97]

These inconceivable figures translate into hundreds of cases where innocent Jews are violently attacked simply because they are Jewish. The wave of incitement includes not only verbal abuse but shocking physical attacks and the destruction of property. Antisemitism often begins in countries where there are almost no Jews. It is easier to incite against us in places where we are almost non-existent in the day-to-day lives of citizens. Jews are used as easy scapegoats and declared the instigators of all that is evil in this world. There is no rhyme or reason for this hate, but for many, it is a way of life.

There is good reason for all people to be concerned about the frightening rise in antisemitism, and unfortunately, it comes from all sides of the political spectrum,[98] not just because it is an evil example of racism and bigotry. Age-old tropes about Jews are consistently dusted off, regurgitated, and spread.[99] Hatred of Jews, when "accepted" and left unchecked, spills over to other forms or ethnic, racial, and demographic hatred. If you allow hate to fester without countering it, people begin to believe the lies and feel justified in acting out. The resulting chaos and violence make the world a dangerous place not just for Jews, but for everyone.

The Challenges Must Be Met with Fortitude

Fighting antisemitism is a challenge, because it isn't predictable. Since it is irrational, we don't know when to expect it, when it will show up, or what the causes are behind it. Because this hatred is on the rise in international institutions like the UN, and not necessarily from our Arab neighbors, fighting it consistently and boldly is a keystone for the Jewish communities' wellbeing. At the UN, I found myself having to point out antisemitism when it happened and also demand that anti-Semitic statements and actions face consequences.

One of my missions, indeed my purpose, is to fight antisemitism at every turn. Israel and other nations need a clear strategy, education, and advocacy to fight this scourge that includes calling out hatred publicly and drafting legislation that punishes perpetrators of hate crimes. As you learned earlier, I didn't hesitate to face off with the director of the Queens Museum who wanted to cancel a historical event. I was successful in doing so, which I hope will inspire others to stand up to bullies and call out inequities and injustices.

At the UN, I found myself in positions of having to call out the hate several times. Rafael Darío Ramírez Carreño, the Venezuelan ambassador to the UN from December 2014 until he was removed from the position on November 28, 2017, was a long-serving bureaucrat and unaccustomed to parsing his words. He was certainly not used to being called on the things he'd say in public forums at the UN. During a discussion in the security council in May 2018, he essentially compared the IDF to the Nazis. "What does Israel plan do to with the Palestinians? Will they disappear? Does Israel seek to wage a final solution? The sort of solution that was perpetrated against the Jews?" Ramirez was referring to the

Nazi's Final Solution, their plan to annihilate the Jewish people, a plan they were partially successful in implementing during the Holocaust. The ambassador from Venezuela made these outrageous remarks one day after Israel marked its annual Holocaust Remembrance Day, which commemorates the six million Jews who were exterminated by the Nazis during the Holocaust.

His words were unacceptable. I could have kept quiet, but I decided to put a red line in the sand about what things can be said against Israel at the UN—and what things cannot stand. Speaking out about it was a gamble worth taking. My character does not permit me to ignore incendiary statements like Ambassador Ramírez's words. Every anti-Semitic remark has to be fought, especially when it is made in a forum that likes to distinguish itself as a respectable place for dignified international dialogue. I started on a low boil, calling other ambassadors to ask if they too would demand a public apology from the ambassador. As a result of my efforts, Ramirez received calls from other ambassadors asking him to apologize.

On the following Friday night, I received a call on my cell phone. As an ambassador, my nights were filled with multiple events. I make every effort to reserve Friday evenings clear so I can have a Shabbat dinner at home with my family and friends. This gives me a chance to disconnect for a few hours from the phone and email. It's our family time and an important Jewish tradition to come together to do a blessing, have dinner, talk about the week, and enjoy each other's company. I am the one who insists that there will be no cell phones on the table during the Shabbat dinner—not an easy task with teenagers in the house. However, on this particular night, I broke my own rule and kept my cell phone turned on, but in a different room. A call came in during dinner. It was from a number I didn't recognize. Something told me to take the call. Ambassador Ramírez was on the line. He started our conversation by telling me that he didn't usually speak with Israelis, but this call was an exception because he wanted to apologize for what he had said in the security council.

"It's very nice of you to make an exception about your policy and call me, Ambassador," I said, "but you have to offer this apology in the same place where you made the statement. The apology is not for me, it is for the Jewish people. It was a verbal attack against my nation." I would accept nothing less than an apology issued in the same room where he had made the ridiculous allegations, in front of the world. "It's the only way to show regret," I added. He told me he would consider it.

After we ended our conversation, I immediately contacted the ambassadors who were active in the apology campaign, and asked them to continue to apply pressure for a public statement. A few days passed, along with much discussion about the remarks. We continued to apply pressure and demand a public apology. Then, on May 12, 2016, Ambassador Ramirez opened his next public remarks at the security council with an apology.[100] He also met with UN Secretary-General Ban Ki-moon's Chef de Cabinet, Edmond Mulet, telling him he regretted using that language. He has a close relationship to the Palestinian leadership, so I am sure it was hard for him, even painful, to make these public statements. For me, it was a successful test that showed that even when you face open hostility and arrogant resistance, if you fight back decisively with a moral coalition, you can make progress.

The Truth About BDS

As I have mentioned, another thorny cause of antisemitism, no matter what its supporters like to say publicly say about it, is the BDS movement, which is active in college and university campuses. People must be educated about what BDS really means, especially impressionable college students. Education and advocacy are key in fighting the scourge of BDS on campuses.

If you know anything about how peer pressure works, along with the pressure from older, powerful academics and tenured professors who are protected from meaningful consequences, you know standing up can be challenging for young people who feel bullied by extremist supporters or BDS activists. It's hard for young people who know BDS is wrong, because BDS activists are emboldened by the support they receive from radical factions inside universities and other public institutions. These students often face hostility and anti-Semitic attacks from fellow students.[101]

As an emissary of The Jewish Agency in the early 1990s, I was fighting BDS even before it had a name. After I graduated from the military service, I explored South America by myself before I started to represent The Jewish Agency on campuses in South Florida. Social media didn't exist at that time, let alone mass-market smartphone technology, so our pro-Israel efforts were grassroots, in person, and local. The anti-Israel movement was not called BDS then; it wasn't organized professionally as it is today, but it was there. I remember setting up a simple folding table on a college campus with the flag of Israel behind me to provide educational flyers about my country. The attacks I received as I stood there remain quite memorable for their viciousness; some students and even some of the tenured professors would shout slurs and ugly threats at us. It wasn't always easy to be the often-lone pro-Israel activist on campus.

One day, I received a phone call from a few students I was friendly with on campus. They told me that Louis Farrakhan of the Nation of Islam was coming to the school for a rally and to deliver a speech. Farrakhan is an anti-Semitic zealot who blames Jews for the American slave trade, plantation slavery, Jim Crow laws, and the general oppression of African Americans.[102] He has conveniently forgotten the involvement of the Jewish community in the Civil Rights movement.[103] He routinely accuses Jews of manipulating the US government and controlling the global levers of power.[104] Together with other students, I helped organize a mass rally against Farrakhan. It was a successful event; we attracted many more students than he did. The main message in the media was that more students came to protest his speech than to listen to it. This is all to say that this issue is in my DNA, and I am always ready to fight anti-Semites or BDS and it goes with me everywhere.

During my tenure at the UN, I made myself available to appear on college campuses. Each time I accepted an invitation to speak, it presented a challenge for my security detail. We often had discussions about whether I should wear a bulletproof vest, which I always declined. Ahead of one heated appearance in 2017 at Columbia University in New York, we had received many threats, which don't deter me. In fact, they do the opposite. Threats make me more determined. On the day of my talk, I told my security detail that because of the noise, threats, and promised violence at the university, we would enter the campus proud and tall through its main gate. No back doors. We would also not allow anyone to disturb my appearance.

There were many protestors for and against Israel outside the hall. Inside the hall, massive groups of students came in with the intention of provocation and disruption. I knew I could handle it, and I don't kowtow to bullies. At the beginning, when I started to speak, the protestors chanted loudly. I made a joke out of them and continued with my speech. I had no fear. I had full confidence in my security detail especially when I learned Munir was assigned to watch my back. Munir came from a Druze village in northern Israel, and he was more than committed to keeping me safe. A large and imposing man, I knew that a college instigator would not be able to get past him. The event was very successful and without further incident.

At the UN, I wanted to find a way to empower students to speak out against BDS on their campuses. One of the efforts I orchestrated was a mega anti-BDS event in the hall of the general assembly. There were several goals for the event: empower students when they get back to their schools, send a message to them that they are not alone and many people are standing together with them against BDS, and draw attention to BDS in the international community. Many ambassadors did not know about BDS and what it seeks to accomplish. I wanted them to know exactly how dangerous and hateful it is.

To be clear, the BDS movement is perverse in the extreme. While it claims to be protesting the policy of the Israeli government, and not against Jewish people or Israeli citizens, many BDS leaders and supporters do hope to eliminate Israel. Palestinian-American journalist Ahmed Moor admits that, "Ending the occupation doesn't mean anything if it doesn't mean upending the Jewish state itself." BDS does mean the end of the Jewish state.[105] Progressive activist John Spritzler has been quite clear about the true aim of BDS, writing, "I think the BDS movement will gain strength from forthrightly explaining why Israel has no right to exist."[106] These activists are not alone.

Finally, I wanted the event to be a wake-up call for Jewish communities and leaders to take action, to be proactive, and recognize that it is a major threat that cannot be ignored.

Organizing the event proved interesting since the UN is typically used as a platform against Israel, not in support of it. I reserved the general assembly hall for the entire day of March 29, 2017. Before doing so, I schooled myself in every UN procedure, including the small print on all its documents regarding events. As a result, I understood that *any* country could reserve the general assembly hall for an event—Israel included. All that is required is that the host country pay expenses and security, which of course, we were more than happy to do.

When we first told the UN administration that the event was specifically anti-BDS, we received push back; the date became mysteriously "unavailable." We revised the event, entitling it on our application, "Building Bridges and Confronting Hate." The official request did not say anything about fighting BDS, but that's what it was. The language we used in the official request was important, and it made it difficult for the UN to say no.

The event was ultimately called "Ambassadors Against BDS." The idea was that we should *all* be ambassadors against BDS. The event was a done deal. Even after we changed its name, the UN could not cancel it.

One of the Jewish leaders I had called about potentially participating told me that having the event was not a good idea. He was concerned that the Palestinians would do a similar event, this one pro-BDS, and also in the general assembly. My reply was that they do it every day, there is no reason for them to rent the hall and pay the expenses. They do it every week, for free. It's not something we need to worry about. And I was right.

We invited thousands of students and Jewish leaders from around the US and Canada, as well as experts from a range of institutions to discuss the damage and wrong-headedness of BDS. It was a remarkable occasion, and another first for the UN. Three thousand people, including two thousand students, came wearing name buttons that said "Stop BDS." Many held Israeli flags. We sang the Israeli anthem, *Hatikvah*, inside the general assembly hall. It was a powerful moment that no participant or observer who was there will forget. For the first time in the UN's history, we created an empowering place for young Jewish people in its halls.

Several high-profile and distinguished guests spoke to the crowd, including Ambassador Nikki Haley; Israeli politician, human rights activist, author, and Soviet refusenik Natan Sharansky; World Jewish Congress President Ronald Lauder; and others. We made sure it would not be seen as a partisan event. It was important to bring together as many representatives of Jewish leadership as possible. Participants and speakers came from both the political left and right, to show solidarity on the issue and work together to fight BDS. We had multiple sessions and panels after the main speaking events.

After the event, I was happily surprised and inspired to hear from ambassadors who told me they had stayed for the entire day, and had learned a great deal about BDS and antisemitism that they had not previously been aware of. It surprised me to know they were not aware of the issue prior to the event but grateful they had learned something new.

The event's goals were fully accomplished. It empowered students from around the world, not just from the US, by giving them the information and tools they needed to fight back. We provided anti-BDS kits they could take with them, which included an Israeli flag and informational flyers they could copy and post in their dormitories, post on school bulletin boards, or distribute at tables. Some of the material included advice and strategies for dealing with various cases of campus BDS and antisemitism, who they can approach, legal resources, and support systems. Moreover, by holding the event in the general assembly at the UN, we sent an unequivocal message that we will not be silent. We are a strong nation, and we will overcome this wave of incitement against Israel. We can win, but in order to win, the State of Israel and world Jewish communities must work together and across political divides to be strong and effective.

It was not easy to pull the event off, not just because of anti-Israeli dissenters at the UN, but because some established Jewish organizations and leaders felt the event would create a backlash. My position is that if you remain quiet, you are an enabler. The fear of backlash is an excuse not to act. Those who disagreed with the event believed that protesting BDS called attention to it and magnified the movement. My view was that BDS was already calling attention to itself and it was gaining traction. Ignoring something doesn't make it go away, it allows it to fester and grow.

Fear and silence do nothing for your cause. We need to expose the issue and talk about what it really means. Students who participated in the event or learned about it saw maybe for the first time that they were not alone. It gave them strength and hope.

Today, the debate is largely over. It is understood that BDS is a problem, and we have to fight it. All major Jewish organizations now have anti-BDS departments, and it has become an important part of their agenda.

Laws are also being passed in the US in order to deter those who promote BDS. Most of the laws are based on the idea of boycotting the boycotters. For instance, the state of Florida can decide not to do business with a business who practices BDS. That is the right approach. As of this writing, thirty-five states, including Alabama, California, Florida, Maine, New York, and others, have adopted laws or policies that prohibit or penalize businesses, organizations, or individuals that engage in or call for boycotts against Israel to one degree or another.[107] The laws or policies in at least seventeen of those states are explicit about companies that refuse to do business in or with Israel.

In January 2019, the US Senate passed a bill[108] that endorsed state anti-boycott legislation, including those that encompass business activity in communities in Judea and Samaria. In March 2019, federal lawmakers introduced resolutions in both the Senate[109] and the House that condemns boycotts of Israel. As of this writing, these initiatives have yet to become US law. There is also legislation in the US regarding federal funding for colleges and universities that support BDS,[110] but it has not as of this writing been signed into law.

Today, BDS is still here and it's not going anywhere. However, you do see more people openly stand against it. There are more resources for students on campuses to fight it. But the BDS' efforts are not going to disappear overnight. We must continue to counter their voices of hate with our own. This struggle is ongoing, which means we are not going to fix it overnight. When I speak to student groups, I tell them when you read history, you see that great victories and successful maneuvers come with persistence. Antisemitism is a chronic illness. It cannot be fixed with surgery but with constant management and treatment. I also compare it to gardening. In order to maintain a beautiful garden, you must weed regularly. You must trim and maintain the plants' structure and health. Fighting BDS and antisemitism is like that. If you forget or reach a level of comfort, cutting back the overgrowth is difficult. It may be too late.

The Equity of Hate

After the March 2019 massacre at the mosque in New Zealand[111] that targeted two mosques and killed forty-nine people, Turkey Prime Minister, Recep Tayyip Erdoğan, instructed his UN ambassador, Selidun Siniloglu, to present a resolution to the general assembly condemning Islamophobia. Erdoğan has always wanted to be seen as the leader of the Muslim world. He believes sponsoring such resolutions puts him in a place of power and respect in the Muslim world. To build his leadership support, he often makes speeches on global issues concerning the Muslim world and sponsors resolutions at the UN that will give him the publicity he craves. There was no condemnation or even footnote on the issue of antisemitism in the draft resolution that Turkey submitted to all the member states. When I read the resolution, I told my staff that it was unacceptable, and we shouldn't allow it to pass as written. The resolution should also include the condemnation of antisemitism.

My staff was skeptical I could make the change, as it was a sensitive issue, especially after such a horrible attack on the mosque. People were understandably upset about what happened. I told them I didn't care about the chances of getting it changed, it's a fight we must engage in. I knew it would have looked bad for Erdoğan to have any opposition or criticism of the resolution, or have it pass without a full consensus. I connected with my allies at the UN and urged them to propose an amendment to the resolution that included a condemnation for antisemitism. This would put pressure on Erdoğan to decide: Put forward the resolution with the original language and take the risk that it would not pass with a consensus, or agree to my language amendment, which would likely pass with a full consensus.

Erdoğan became personally involved in the discussion. He was unwilling to change the wording. It became a poker game between him and me. I spoke to more countries in the EU. The more people I reached to explain my position, the more support I built. It wasn't easy, because many countries didn't want to argue about a sensitive issue especially coming on the heels of the attack of the mosque. Some EU officials tried to convince me to drop it. Their idea was to draft a separate resolution condemning antisemitism that would be brought up at a future date. I had enough experience in these instances to know that tomorrow never comes. Even if an EU official can guarantee the EU votes, he cannot guarantee the vote of the other members in the general assembly. I declined the offer.

Instead, I went to the US, Canada, and the other strong friends of Israel to try to convince them it was not appropriate. I was tested; two friendly ambassadors came to me and said that while they supported my position, perhaps it was not a good idea to pursue it because the timing was bad. "Perhaps we should not fight it," they told me. "If it's put forward, it's important not to vote against it, it's not such a bad thing to condemn Islamophobia."

I had to play poker even with my friends in this instance. I told colleagues who were supporting my efforts that even if they backed down and I was left alone, I would enter the GA and vote against it. They knew I was capable of doing it. I held all the cards close to the vest. No one knew what orders I received from Jerusalem. They didn't know it was not to vote against the Turkish resolution if it came to a vote. No one knew that but me. My colleagues informed the EU ambassadors and other major players at the UN of my thoughts. That message got to Erdoğan very quickly. The strategy worked. Erdoğan chose to agree to the inclusion of the condemnation of antisemitism in the resolution. It was proof that if you stick to your principles, and you are willing to lose, you can achieve historic victories.

In June 2019, there was a wave of anti-Semitic incidents around the world, including the incident I described earlier, when a gunman opened fire at the Chabad of Poway synagogue, outside San Diego, on the last day of Passover, one of the holiest holidays in the Jewish calendar.[112] I initiated a special event about antisemitism at the UN General Assembly. Some member states wanted to shift this event to a broader discussion of Islamophobia and xenophobia. I didn't accept this. As I discussed earlier, when you look at the actual numbers of hate crimes, you see a different story than what is sometimes presented in the news.

Globally, anti-Semitic hate crimes comprise the number one hate crime. I had to convince many at the UN to hold this discussion in the original format. I faced opposition, as always, from some European countries. We have very strong friends in Europe, but some in the EU are often problematic and oppose anything which is favorable for Israel. The EU is an important group, because many other smaller and less powerful groups follow their decisions and vote as they do. I did get support from friends in Eastern Europe, but there were others from Western Europe who were quite vocal against my initiative. To overcome the opposition, I asked to come to the weekly meeting of the EU ambassadors. I had five minutes to make my case to these individuals, some of whom are less than friendly toward Israel. I took a very direct approach.

My words and points were focused on those who were leading the opposition. I told them that we expected them to stand with us on this issue—with no ifs, ands, or buts. I was asked whether the event could include other forms of hate crimes. I told them if that was the case, we would not participate in the event. The EU ambassador tried to push for a compromise, and he asked why we could not simply have a discussion about confronting hate crimes, but I did not relent. I was not shy about it. I looked them in the eyes and told them they were not in a position to block the debate in the general assembly against antisemitism not only because of the past, but because of what is going on in their own countries in the present. When I delivered my strong concluding remarks, I looked directly at the ambassador from Ireland, one of the leading voices against my initiative.

I was then asked to leave the room, so the group could discuss and vote on this issue. The majority supported me, and eventually the EU decided to support the event without extending it beyond antisemitism. More than ninety countries participated including Syria, Egypt, Morocco, Turkey, and Iran. Representatives from Jewish and pro-Israel organizations were also in attendance, as was the EU Commission Coordinator for combating antisemitism, Katharina von Schnurbein. Perhaps the most compelling participants were victims of anti-Semitic hate crimes, including Rabbi Yisroel Goldstein, who was injured in the Poway shooting. He was joined by the daughter and sister of Lori Gilbert Kaye, who was killed in the attack.

The event made an impression on everyone who attended, including the secretary general, UN officials, and many ambassadors. It was held in a forum that was not often, if ever, used to discuss anti-Semitic and hate crimes against Jews. I was proud of that moment and the hard work I did that allowed Rabbi Goldstein and others to talk about the resilience and fortitude of the Jewish people.

Partly as a result of this event, in October 2019,[113] the UN issued its first ever important and thorough report dedicated wholly to antisemitism.[114] It is important to note that the UN also passed a definition of antisemitism, which includes anti-Zionism. It was submitted to the general assembly by UN special rapporteur on freedom of religion, Ahmed Shaheed.

Unify for Peace & Strength

Antisemitism will not disappear. Outspokenness, education, advocacy, activism, and legislation are important, as I've demonstrated here. However, in times of crisis, we must also put ephemeral political disagreements aside and unite. The mutual responsibility that exists between Israel and World Jewry is clear. The connection between Jews and Israel, which is a force multiplier for us, is also used by our enemies. Iran's supreme leader, Ali Khamenei, is not only opposed to Israel, he also detests Jews. He labels the Jewish people "dogs," "inhuman," and other such insulting and abusive terms. This is called "othering"[115] and he is not alone in this practice. In Syria and even in Egypt, a country with whom Israel has a peace agreement, too many are still involved in antisemitism and Holocaust denial.

Israeli citizens also have a duty to find bigger and better ways to increase solidarity with World Jewry. It shouldn't simply be about assisting Jews or helping those who recently arrived in Israel. We must also stand shoulder to shoulder with our Jewish communities worldwide. We have not yet achieved this goal completely and must strive to do so. We must ensure this idea becomes enshrined in public policy and part of international discourse. It is crucial that we all continue to intensify our global efforts in the war against antisemitism.

We must also continue with legislative and punitive activity in all countries against perpetrators of hate crimes, as has been done in Germany and Austria, for example. We must call for the enactment of explicit laws against anti-Semitic acts and demonstrate our collective strength in the face of irrational and violent action. Israel must demand from each country that it protect its Jewish citizens and act resolutely and swiftly against any manifestation of antisemitism. The demand should be assertive and heard everywhere, at all times.

The Peace Process

Israel has to participate in the peace process actively and continuously, even when there are those who refuse to come to the table. Any negotiation should be based on the recognition of the state of Israel. Many times, we Israelis feel as if the debate is not about any concrete issues, but rather, about our right to exist in the land of Israel.

A reliable plan must recognize that the situation today in Israel, the Palestinian Authority, and the broader Middle East, has changed dramatically from the beginning of the peace process, which began in the 1990s.

In the past quarter of a century, the Middle East has devolved into instability. The Iranian regime has significantly expanded its regional operations and, buoyed by the windfall from the nuclear deal, has spent $7 billion per year on its terror network, including $1 billion a year to Hezbollah on Israel's northern border.[116] Tehran's support for the Assad regime has prolonged the Syrian civil war and allowed the Iranians to position their troops near the Israeli and Jordanian borders.[117]

The rise of the Islamic State and its sudden expansion from Iraq into Syria shocked the region, proving that power vacuums enable non-state actors to establish a base of operations from which they can threaten their host nations and neighboring states. The presence of the Islamic State and al-Qaeda affiliates in the Sinai Peninsula is further evidence of this point.

Within the Palestinian body politic, the Palestinian Authority lost control of the Gaza Strip in a bloody civil war to Hamas, the internationally recognized terrorist organization, in 2006. The strip is now home to numerous terrorist organizations, supported and funded by Iran to the tune of up to $100 million per year.[118] The result has been thousands of mortars, rockets, and missiles fired into Israeli civilian centers in the past fifteen years.[119]

It is abundantly clear that the Middle East has irrevocably changed over the past twenty-five years. Perhaps the best evidence of this change is the forging of new relationships that were impossible to imagine even a decade ago. In 2016, I visited the United Arab Emirates; in October 2018, Prime Minister Benjamin Netanyahu met with Sultan Qaboos bin Said in Oman[120]; and last summer, Bahrain hosted the "Peace to Prosperity" conference.[121] All three countries' ambassadors were present in the White House as President Trump presented the Abraham Accords.

Yet despite the dramatic changes in the region's political and security dynamics, some still embrace the old political solution codified in the 1993 Oslo Accords.[122] Applying a 1990s solution to today's environment is a mistake. It is like insisting everyone continue using a pager in the era of smartphones. Any viable plan will provide the opportunity for the Palestinians to build the necessary institutions they currently lack. Multiple initiatives focus on ensuring effective governance, expanding the Palestinian educational and healthcare systems and, perhaps most notably, guaranteeing foreign investment.[123] Imagine what Palestinian society could achieve with such opportunities!

Only President Mahmoud Abbas and the Palestinian Authority would have the chutzpah to continue to reject any opportunity.

In ignoring history and the changing realities, some international players continue to condemn Israel and repeat the results of the last quarter-century of failed peace efforts. This exemplifies the popular definition of insanity: repeating the same formula—which failed at Oslo in 1993, at Camp David in 2000, and with Ehud Olmert's offer in 2008—but expecting a different result.

It is time to accept that the new reality in the Middle East requires adopting new solutions. My hope is that the Biden administration does not doom Israel and the Palestinian people by returning to the old paradigms and the mistakes of the past.

I also worry about the Iran nuclear deal, the Joint Comprehensive Plan of Action (JCPOA), and it is my hope that the

Biden administration does not opt to rejoin the agreement. They know the flaws of the agreement; we have outlined them publicly many times in the past, including in front of the security council at the UN.

Allowances for certain Iranian ballistic missile activities, uranium enrichment, continued support for regional militias and so-called "sunset clauses" that roll back selected restrictions against Iran are just some of the obvious shortcomings of the deal. The situation in Iran has worsened since 2015, and if the US decides to reenter into the original Obama-era Iran deal without amendments, Israel will have tough decisions to make toward Iran. The Iran of 2021 is not the Iran of 2016. Today, they are in a much more advanced condition, unfortunately. We cannot pretend that things remain the same.

In order to continue to live safely and achieve lasting peace, we should continue to seek new partners in the region, and around the globe while maintaining our autonomy. One might think that there is an inherent contradiction between these two goals. In this book, I prove not only that it is possible to have full sovereignty and independence around crucial decisions related to our security while simultaneously enhancing existing relationships and reaching out to more countries and players to build new bridges—it is essential.

We are living in a unique era and should be grateful for what we have achieved in our young and vibrant country. We should not take for granted the remarkable society we have built in a challenging and demanding region. With the same passion and determination, we will continue to move forward and strengthen the only national home of the Jewish people.

"May G-d give strength unto His people;
May G-d bless His people with peace."
Psalms 29:11

ACKNOWLEDGMENTS

After completing my first book, *Israel: The Will to Prevail* in 2012, I told my wife, Talie, that I thought it would be my first book, and also my last. However, after an intense and dramatic five years at the UN, I felt I had to share the experiences I had there and how it has further crystalized my vision for the future of Israel.

My journey to public life and my involvement representing the country I love so much started at a very young age. When I was sixteen, I was chosen to be part of an Israeli youth delegation exchange program to the US and Canada. As part of our trip, we visited the UN. I took the advantage of the opportunity to send a postcard to my mother describing my visit to the building. Once I assumed the distinguished position of Israel's Ambassador to the UN, my mother found the old postcard and framed it for me.

I will always be grateful for my mother, Yocheved Danon, who, despite her challenging life, found the enormous power to instill in me the self-confidence to stand proud and tall while I make my case on any issue. I still remember when I was ten years old, coming back from school after an ideological argument with one of my teachers about the role of the underground movement pre-Israel's independence. The teacher was not happy that I embarrassed him publicly with facts, and he demanded to hear from my parents. He did not expect to receive a very polite but direct letter from my mother explaining that she supported my views. I will never forget the expression on his face while reading her letter. After my father passed away, despite her young age, she chose not to open a second chapter in her life but instead dedicated her life to her children and, later, her grandchildren. I will always love you and remember your inner strength and the support you gave me, like a lioness protecting her youngest cub.

Relocation of a family, especially one of significant distance in terms of both miles and cultures, is fraught with difficulties and challenges. In our case, it brought us together in dealing with the unknown, which provided us with an amazing experience as a family.

To my wife, Talie, the love of my life and best friend for the last twenty-five years, I know how hard you work to bring up our amazing children and I admire your patience for my ideas, even when they seem unachievable. I know that when you stand by my side anything is possible. During our tenure in New York City, I was amazed to see the skills you developed in building bridges and representing Israel. Your creative ideas proved to be the best PR for our beloved country. You proved to be an amazing Ambassador for the state of Israel and the Jewish people. I am sure that many of the diplomats we introduced to Israel and the Jewish tradition will cherish the Shabbat dinners you hosted and the great time we had during the missions to Israel. God-willing, our next twenty-five years will be just as exciting and rewarding.

To my oldest son, Aviad Joseph, you are named after your legendary grandfather, Joseph Danon. I am sure he would have been very proud of you. You left behind your friends in Israel and despite the challenges of moving to New York, you were able to excel in school and build amazing new friendships. I admire your ability to communicate naturally and sincerely with everyone, whether they be a head of state or a taxi driver.

Upon our arrival to New York, we escorted our daughter, Hila, to meet her teacher, Josh, a day before the school opened. Only after we met did we realize that he didn't speak any Hebrew at all! Hila was eleven years old at the time and spoke only very basic English. Josh wasn't sure how he could teach English literature to someone who didn't speak English. Talie and I smiled, knowing Hila and her strong character. It would not be an issue. Three months later, Hila was writing impressive essays in English. Hila, you have a strong and independent character. I'm sure you will achieve all the goals you will set for yourself in the future. I have no doubt that the light you bring to our family will shine on many others.

Shira, my youngest daughter, is the youngest sibling in my family, as am I, so I know how challenging it can be. You prove that still waters run deep. In your unique way, you adjusted to a new environment once in New York City and again, upon our return to Israel. Shira, thank you for all of your support and the encouragement you give me.

Special thanks to my in-laws, Shalom and Dina, who took a major part in the upbringing of our children. While we were in Israel you covered us during the time I held very demanding public positions. Despite the distance and the time difference you were there for our children even when we were in the US. You visited us so many times and thanks to modern technology, we were able to participate in your Friday night services remotely. As you know, it was not the same, since it was still afternoon in New York City and we could only see the great dishes that Dina prepared for Shabbat.

On one occasion, Talie and I were looking for a babysitter that would stay with the children for three days while I participated in a few events on the west coast. We were shocked to learn the cost of such care, and realized it would be less expensive to fly Shalom from Israel. When we called him, he didn't hesitate. He was on the plane and was the best babysitter my children could hope for.

I am grateful to my brother, Eyal, and my sister, Shirly, and their beautiful families who came to visit us and spend unforgettable times with us during those visits. We found out that only when we had guests coming over from Israel did we actually take the time to explore the great attractions of New York City.

In this book, I describe the great achievements and some of the amazing events we held during my term as Israel's Ambassador to the UN. While I take the credit for the successes and responsibility for the failures, I have no words to thank the great team that stood by my side. A devoted group of young, committed Zionists were there on the frontlines, day and night, preparing the events and speeches, and coordinating hundreds of media interviews. During the long nights we stayed up working, I used to tell you that one day you will be able to share with your grandchildren what you were doing at the mission. I will always be grateful for the great advice you offered, and your service on behalf of the State of Israel.

Some days I spent more time with my security detail than with my own family. I always knew they had my back, whether it was in the car, during a crowded event, or in a jog in central park. Rain or shine, you were there, willing to step in and neutralize any threat and for that I am grateful. In every position I entered in my career, I always found the one or two team members who knew everybody and everything. In our case, we found Daisy, the house manager, to be a real asset. She helped us blend in and when we hosted events in our apartment she was able to coordinate everything. This is no small challenge when you have to follow demanding protocol. I developed a tradition of hosting Ambassadors for breakfasts in my home almost every week. Together with Daisy, we introduced them to Israeli salad and spicy shakshuka. Food is the best ice breaker one can find.

Another devoted member of our team was my driver, Robert, who worked with many of my predecessors. Robert knew every corner of the city and we trusted him and his advice. I promised him that once he realized his dream to visit Israel, I would be his driver through the streets of Jerusalem.

Writing a book like this does not happen in a vacuum. I would like to thank Karen Kelly, who worked with me on this book and captured my words. Thank you Karen for your friendship. Special thanks to Carol Mann, my literary agent for her wisdom and experience. Many thanks to Adam Bellow and the great team at Post Hill Press for their support.

One of the advantages of assuming a diplomatic post is the chance to meet new people from all around the world. I am grateful for the new friendships I made with so many unique and special individuals. To Ambassador Nikki Haley, who is a close friend of Talie and myself, thank you for the inspiring forward to this book, and thank you for being a true friend of the state of Israel.

Last but definitely not least, I would like to extend my humble gratitude to the Israeli people and the Jewish communities around the world for giving me the unique opportunity to represent the Jewish people on the stage of the United Nations. I will cherish that opportunity and will make the best of the knowledge I gained to continue to serve my people with pride and determination.

ENDNOTES

1   Improvate, "Israeli Technology Leading World Out of COVID-19 Crisis," PR Newswire, January 25, 2021, https://www.prnewswire.com/news-releases/israeli-technology-leading-world-out-of-covid-19-crisis-301213942.html.

2   "Israel's Benjamin Netanyahu agrees coalition deal," BBC News, May 7, 2015, https://www.bbc.com/news/world-middle-east-32618192.

3   David Horovitz, "Danny Danon, dismally, is the true face of Netanyahu's Israel," The Times of Israel, August 14, 2015, https://www.timesofisrael.com/danny-danon-dismally-is-the-true-face-of-netanyahus-israel/.

4   Allison Kaplan Sommer, "Six Reasons to Worry About Israel's New UN Ambassador Danny Danon," Haaretz, last modified April 10, 2018, https://www.haaretz.com/.premium-six-reasons-to-worry-about-israels-new-un-ambassador-1.5387895.

5   Herb Keinon, "Danny Danon appointment shows what Netanyahu thinks of UN," The Jerusalem Post, last modified August 16, 2015, https://www.jpost.com/israel-news/politics-and-diplomacy/new-ambassador-to-un-danon-pledges-to-surprise-his-critics-412221.

6   Daniel Gordis, "Making Sense of Israel's Odd UN Appointment," *Bloomberg*, August 18, 2015, https://www.bloomberg.com/opinion/articles/2015-08-18/making-sense-of-israel-s-odd-un-appointment.

7   Jodi Rudoren, "Netanyahu Appoints Right-Wing Politician as Israeli Ambassador to U.N.," *The New York Times,* August 14, 2015, https://www.nytimes.com/2015/08/15/world/middleeast/netanyahu-appoints-right-wing-politician-as-israeli-ambassador-to-un.html.

8   "Israel Population 2021 (Live)," World Population Review, https://worldpopulationreview.com/countries/israel-population.

9   "By My Spirit," Holy Land Moments, June 9, 2017, https://www.holylandmoments.ca/devotionals/by-my-spirit-3.

10 "Prime Minister Winston Churchill's address to Harrow School on October 29, 1941," University of Waterloo, http://www.eng.uwaterloo.ca/~jcslee/poetry/churchill_nevergivein.html.

11 Zeke J. Miller, "Transcript: Netanyahu Speech to Congress," *Time,* March 3, 2015, https://time.com/3730318/transcript-netanyahu-speech-to-congress/.

12 AssafChriqui, "Israeli Ambassador full speech on UN settlement vote (UNSC Resolution 2334)," YouTube, 5:56, December 23, 2016, https://www.youtube.com/watch?v=hPxSx8qdpWA.

13 "Full Text of Obama's UN General Assembly Speech," Haaretz, September 24, 2013, https://www.haaretz.com/1.5180811.

14 Kambiz Froohar, "Jerusalem Embassy Vote Draws First U.S. Veto at UN Under Trump," *Bloomberg,* December 17, 2017, https://www.bloomberg.com/news/articles/2017-12-17/un-to-vote-on-resolution-rejecting-trump-jerusalem-embassy-move.

15 Bari Weiss, "Can an Archaeological Dig Change the Future of Jerusalem?" *The New York Times*, March 30, 2019, https://www.nytimes.com/interactive/2019/03/30/opinion/sunday/jerusalem-city-of-david-israel-dig.html.

16   Countries voting against the resolution were Togo,
      Micronesia, Nauru, Palau, Marshall Islands, Guatemala
      and Honduras.

17   Abstaining countries included Antigua-Barbuda, Argentina,
      Australia, the Bahamas, Benin, Bhutan, Bosnia-Herzegovina,
      Cameroon, Canada, Colombia, Croatia, Czech Republic,
      Dominican Republic, Equatorial Guinea, Fiji, Haiti, Hungary,
      Jamaica, Kiribati, Latvia, Lesotho, Malawi, Mexico, Panama,
      Paraguay, the Philippines, Poland, Romania, Rwanda, the
      Solomon Islands, South Sudan, Trinidad and Tobago, Tuvalu,
      Uganda, and Vanuatu. Amanda Connolly, "Canada among 35
      abstaining from UN vote condemning American embassy
      move to Jerusalem," Global News, December 21, 2017,
      https://globalnews.ca/news/3929255/canada-abstains-un-vote-
      american-embassy-jerusalem/.

18   I want to point out that while many observers, including
      reporters, were convinced that the Palestinian protests that
      took place on May 14 and 15 were a direct result of the
      Embassy opening; it really was in the context of the
      so-called Great March of Return, a six-week campaign
      launched by Hamas and other Palestinian groups which
      began in late March and reached a peak on May 14, one day
      before the Gregorian day marking Israel's 70th anniversary,
      which the Palestinians call Nakba Day (or Catastrophe Day).

19   Vanessa Friedman, "The Power of the Yellow Vest," *The New
      York Times,* December 4, 2018, https://www.nytimes.
      com/2018/12/04/fashion/yellow-vests-france-protest-
      fashion.html.

20   Jonathan Cook, "Israel's choice of envoy sends a message to
      the UN," The National News, August 24, 2015, https://www.
      thenationalnews.com/opinion/israel-s-choice-of-envoy-
      sends-a-message-to-the-un-1.14608/.

21   Jonathan Cook, "Just as Dermer turned the White House
      into a diplomatic battlefield, Danon will do the same at the

UN," Mondoweiss, August 25, 2015, https://mondoweiss. net/2015/08/turned-diplomatic-battlefield/.

22 Batsheva Sobelman, "Palestinian goes on trial in stabbing attack on fellow 13-year-old," *The Los Angeles Times,* November 10, 2015, https://www.latimes.com/world/ middleeast/la-fg-israel-palestinians-stabbings-teen-20151110-story.html.

23 Steven Erlanger, "Tearfully but Forcefully, Israel Removes Gaza Settlers," *The New York Times,* August 18, 2005, https://www.nytimes.com/2005/08/18/world/middleeast/ tearfully-but-forcefully-israel-removes-gaza-settlers.html.

24 The Group of 77, "Latest Statements and Speeches," The Group of 77 at the United Nations, http://www.g77.org.

25 Fiamma Nirenstein, "Erdoğan uses incitement as an ideological weapon of war," Jewish News Syndicate, November 1, 2020, https://www.jns.org/opinion/ erdogan-uses-incitement-as-an-ideological-weapon-of-war/.

26 Seth J. Frantzman, "Analysis: Turkey's Erdogan stakes his claim to Jerusalem," The Jerusalem Post, last modified May 10, 2017, https://www.jpost.com/Israel-News/Analysis-Erdogan-stakes-his-claim-to-Jerusalem-490217.

27 Raphael Ahern, "'Jerusalem is our city,' Turkey's Erdogan declares," The Times of Israel, October 1, 2020, https:// www.timesofisrael.com/jerusalem-is-our-city-turkeys-erdogan-declares/.

28 Yoni Weiss, "Report: Turkey Willing to Exchange Ambassadors With Israel," Hamodia, March 30, 2021, https://hamodia.com/2021/03/30/ report-turkey-willing-exchange-ambassadors-israel/.

29 Yoni Weiss, "Israel Denies Turkish Request for Ambassadorial Exchange," Hamodia, March 30, 2021, https://hamodia.com/2021/03/30/israel-denies-turkish-request-ambassadorial-exchange/.

30 Saeed Abdulrazzak, "Turkey Orders Muslim Brotherhood
    TV Channels to Stop Attacking Egypt," Asharq Al-Awsat,
    March 20, 2021, https://english.aawsat.com/home/
    article/2870866/turkey-orders-muslim-brotherhood-tv-
    channels-stop-attacking-egypt.

31 Brent Scher, "Donald Trump's U.N Pick Was First Governor
    to Sign Anti-BDS Legislation," The Washington Free Beacon,
    November 23, 2016, https://freebeacon.com/issues/donald-
    trumps-u-n-pick-was-first-governor-to-sign-anti-bds-
    legislation/.

32 Nikki Haley, *With All Due Respect* (New York: St Martin's
    Press, 2019, p.99).

33 Shaina Oppenheimer, "'A Life-and-death Matter': How Israel
    Helped Singapore When It Needed It Most," Haaretz, March
    16, 2020, https://www.haaretz.com/israel-news/.premium-
    the-lion-city-and-the-start-up-nation-how-israel-helped-
    singapore-1.8676074.

34 Merrit Kennedy, "For First Time, U.S. Abstains On U.N.
    Resolution Criticizing Cuba Embargo," NPR, October 26,
    2016, https://www.npr.org/sections/thetwo-way/2016/10/
    26/499469386/for-first-time-u-s-abstains-on-u-n-resolution-
    condemning-cuba-embargo.

35 Glick, Edward B., "Palestine Partition Resolution," Journal of
    Inter-American Studies Vol. 1, No. 2 (Apr., 1959), pp.
    211-222 (12 pages), Cambridge University Press, https://
    www.jstor.org/stable/165028.

36 Jeffrey Heller and Dan Williams, "Guatemala opens embassy
    in Jerusalem, two days after U.S. move," Reuters, May 16,
    2018,https://www.reuters.com/article/us-israel-palestinians-
    guatemala-idUSKCN1IH0Q7.

37 Pedro Servin, "Paraguay moves Israel embassy back out of
    Jerusalem," AP News, September 5, 2018, https://apnews.
    com/article/47777edc22f548e4a8f69fd239f0e6ef.

[38] Ali Sawafta and Daniela Desantis, "Israel closing embassy in Paraguay in response to return of mission to Tel Aviv," Reuters, September 5, 2018, https://www.reuters.com/article/us-paraguay-israel-netanyahu/israel-closing-embassy-in-paraguay-in-response-to-return-of-mission-to-tel-aviv-idUSKCN1LL2KG.

[39] Ilan Ben Zion, "Honduras opens embassy in Jerusalem, 4th country to do so," AP News, June 24, 2021, https://apnews.com/article/donald-trump-jerusalem-honduras-middle-east-religion-49d8f0a908d2a0bf16830071e2c6f5f0.

[40] Ilan Ben Zion, "Honduras opens embassy in Jerusalem, 4th country to do so," AP News, June 24, 2021, https://apnews.com/article/donald-trump-jerusalem-honduras-middle-east-religion-49d8f0a908d2a0bf16830071e2c6f5f0.

[41] Zenel Zhinipotoku and Llazar Semini, "Kosovo opens embassy to Israel in Jerusalem," AP News, March 14, 2021, https://apnews.com/article/europe-embassies-israel-kosovo-summits-451d3caf98fac4ed37abcd74e6815a8a.

[42] Barak Ravid, "Days After Netanyahu-Putin Meeting, Russia Threatened to Veto anti-Hezbollah Move Led by Israel and U.S. at UN," Haaretz, September 6, 2017, https://www.haaretz.com/israel-news/russia-threatened-to-veto-anti-hezbollah-move-at-un-1.5448254.

[43] "Lebanese parties must not get involved in Syrian crisis, Security Council stresses," United Nations News, March 14, 2013, https://news.un.org/en/story/2013/03/434452-lebanese-parties-must-not-get-involved-syrian-crisis-security-council-stresses.

[44] "Security Council Committee pursuant to resolutions 1267 (1999) 1989 (2011) and 2253 (2015) concerning Islamic State in Iraq and the Levant (Da'esh), Al-Qaida and associated individuals, groups, undertakings and entities," United Nations Security Council, https://www.un.org/securitycouncil/sanctions/1267.

45   Alexander Corbeil, "Hezbollah is Learning Russian,"
      Carnegie Endowment for International Peace, February 26,
      2016, https://carnegieendowment.org/sada/62896?lang=en.

46   Associated Press, "Israel gains a seat on U.N. panel after 50
      years of isolation," Deseret News, May 31, 2000, https://
      www.deseret.com/2000/5/31/19560460/
      israel-gains-a-seat-on-u-n-panel-after-50-years-of-isolation.

47   Associated Press, "Israel pulls out of race for seat on UN
      security council," The Guardian, May 5, 2018, https://www.
      theguardian.com/world/2018/may/05/israel-pulls-out-of-
      race-for-seat-on-un-security-council.

48   "US resolution to condemn activities of Hamas voted down
      in General Assembly," United Nations News, December 6,
      2018, https://news.un.org/en/story/2018/12/1027881.

49   JB Shreve, "Israel Has A Right to Defend Itself—This Is Not
      Defense," JBShreve.com, May 19, 2021, https://jbshreve.
      medium.com/israel-has-a-right-to-defend-itself-this-is-
      not-defense-8b462396837b.

50   Yagil Levy, "Israel's Iron Dome defense system protects
      Israeli lives. It also perpetuates the Israel-Gaza conflict," The
      Washington Post, May 14, 2021, https://www.
      washingtonpost.com/politics/2021/05/14/israels-iron-dome-
      defense-system-protects-israeli-lives-it-also-perpetuates-
      israel-gaza-conflict/.

51   Aryeh Savir, "Israel slams UN's 'shameful' war crimes
      probe," World Israel News, May 30, 2021, https://
      worldisraelnews.com/israel-slams-uns-shameful-war-
      crimes-probe/.

52   Reuters, "Israel begins operation to expose Hezbollah 'attack
      tunnels' on Lebanon border," The Guardian, December 4,
      2018, https://www.theguardian.com/world/2018/dec/04/
      israel-military-hezbollah-attack-tunnels-lebanon-border.

53   Times of Israel staff and Judah Ari Gross, "IDF reveals
      'longest, most significant' Hezbollah tunnel on northern

border," The Times of Israel, last modified May 30, 2019, https://www.timesofisrael.com/idf-reveals-longest-most-significant-hezbollah-tunnel-yet-on-northern-border/.

54   Fares Akram and Josef Federman, "58 dead in Gaza protests as Israel fetes US Embassy move," AP News, May 15, 2018, https://apnews.com/article/donald-trump-ap-top-news-international-news-hamas-jerusalem-42e68289e3244ca2879 f258d4e445850.

55   Nitsan Keidar, "Danon chides France in maiden UN speech," Israel National News, October 22, 2015, https://www. israelnationalnews.com/News/News.aspx/202311.

56   World Tribune, "'Israeli blood is no less valuable than French blood,' Danon tells UN," World Tribune, November 24, 2015, https://www.worldtribune.com/archives/ israeli-blood-is-no-less-valuable-than-french-blood-danon-tells-un/.

57   Ari Yashar, "'Peaceful resistance'? PA, Fatah call to stab Jews," Israel National News, October 22, 2015, https://www. israelnationalnews.com/News/News.aspx/202295.

58   Zalman Ahnsaf, "Annual Israel-Bashing Day at U.N.," Hamodia, December 1, 2016, https://hamodia.com/2016/ 12/01/annual-israel-bashing-day-u-n/.

59   Judah Ari Gross, "Israel charges UN employee with aiding Hamas in Gaza," The Times of Israel, August 9, 2016, https://www.timesofisrael.com/israel-charges-un-employee-with-aiding-hamas-in-gaza/.

60   "Charter of the United Nations: Chapter XVI—Miscellaneous Provisions," Codification Division Publications, https:// legal.un.org/repertory/art104_105.shtml.

61   Ariane Mandell and Herb Keinon, "Danon denies UN prisoner release demands, stating 'Immunity is not given to terrorists'," The Jerusalem Post, last modified August 25, 2016, https://m.jpost.com/arab-israeli-conflict/

danon-denies-un-prisoner-release-demands-stating-
immunity-is-not-given-to-terrorists-466098/amp.

62   Reuters, "Israel sentences Palestinian UN worker for aiding
     Hamas in plea deal," Eyewitness News, January 5, 2017,
     https://ewn.co.za/2017/01/05/israel-sentences-palestinian-
     un-worker-for-aiding-hamas-in-plea-deal.

63   Anna Kokko, "For ordinary Palestinians, full support of BDS
     is impossible," Albawaba News, June 25, 2015, https://www.
     albawaba.com/business/ordinary-palestinians-full-support-
     bds-impossible-712178; Jake Wallis Simon, "Why even the
     Palestinian Authority opposes the boycott of Israel ?,"
     Europe Israel Press Association, June 11, 2014, https://eipa.
     eu.com/2014/06/why-even-the-palestinian-authority-
     opposes-the-boycott-of-israel/.

64   United Nations, "Report on UNCTAD assistance to the
     Palestinian people: Developments in the economy of the
     Occupied Palestinian Territory," United Nations Conference
     on Trade and Development, July 22, 2019, https://unctad.
     org/system/files/official-document/tdbex68d4_en.pdf.

65   Lucy Garbett, "Palestinian Workers in Israel Caught
     Between Indispensable and Disposable," Middle East
     Research and Information Project, May 15, 2020, https://
     merip.org/2020/05/palestinian-workers-in-israel-caught-
     between-indispensable-and-disposable/#_edn1.

66   Yoel Goldman, "Abbas: Don't boycott Israel," The Times of
     Israel, December 13, 2013, https://www.timesofisrael.com/
     abbas-we-do-not-support-the-boycott-of-israel/.

67   Kareem Estefan, Carin Kuoni, and Laura Raicovich,
     "*Assuming Boycott: Resistance, Agency and Cultural
     Production*," October 10, 2017, https://www.amazon.com/
     Assuming-Boycott-Resistance-Cultural-Production/dp/
     1944869433/ref=sr_1_1?dchild=1&keywords=assuming+
     boycott&qid=1626040322&sr=8-1.

68   Kareem Estefan, Carin Kuoni, and Laura Raicovich. "FOREWORD." *Assuming Boycott: Resistance, Agency, and Cultural Production* (New York; London: OR Books, 2017, pp. 7–10). *JSTOR*, www.jstor.org/stable/j.ctv62hfrq.3. Accessed 19 Mar. 2020.

69   Gloria Pazmino, "Queens Museum reinstates Israel event after backlash," Politico, August 16, 2017, https://www.politico.com/states/new-york/city-hall/story/2017/08/16/queens-museum-reconsidering-israel-event-cancellation-after-backlash-113992.

70   Gloria Pazmino, "Queens Museum reinstates Israel event after backlash," Politico, August 16, 2017, https://www.politico.com/states/new-york/city-hall/story/2017/08/16/queens-museum-reconsidering-israel-event-cancellation-after-backlash-113992.

71   Andy Battaglia, "Laura Raicovich Counters Queens Museum Report of 'Poor Judgement' and Misleading Board," ARTnews, February 15, 2018, https://www.artnews.com/art-news/news/laura-raicovich-counters-queens-museum-report-poor-judgement-misleading-board-9822/.

72   "Israeli Practices towards the Palestinian People and the Question of Apartheid," United Nations ESCWA, March 2017, https://electronicintifada.net/sites/default/files/2017-03/un_apartheid_report_15_march_english_final_.pdf.

73   "Economy of Israel," Fanack.com, June 6, 2020, https://fanack.com/israel/economy-of-israel/.

74   "Gross domestic spending on R&D," OECD Data, https://data.oecd.org/rd/gross-domestic-spending-on-r-d.htm.

75   Michelle Jamrisko, Lee J. Miller, and Wei Lu, "These Are the World's Most Innovative Countries," Bloomberg, January 22, 2019, https://www.bloomberg.com/news/articles/2019-01-22/germany-nearly-catches-korea-as-innovation-champ-u-s-rebounds.

76   Rabbi Steven Carr Reuben, "Imagine a World Without Israel - Part 2," Huffpost, last modified October 24, 2014, https://www.huffpost.com/entry/imagine-a-world-without-i_1_b_5706935.

77   "Gross Domestic Product," Google, last modified April 8, 2020, https://www.google.com/publicdata/explore?ds=d5bncppjof8f9_&met_y=ny_gdp_mktp_cd&idim=country:ISR&dl=en&hl=en&q=israel+gdp.

78   Debbie Buchwald, "Israel's High-Tech Boom," Jewish Policy Center, Summer 2008, https://www.jewishpolicycenter.org/2008/05/31/israels-high-tech-boom/.

79   "Israel Economy," The Heritage Foundation, https://www.heritage.org/index/country/israel.

80   David Axe, "Turkey Is The Middle East's Newest Drone Super Power," The National Interest, April 9, 2020, https://nationalinterest.org/blog/buzz/turkey-middle-easts-newest-drone-super-power-142242.

81   Charlie Gao, "Why Loitering Munitions Are the Newest and Deadliest Threat," The National Interest, September 17, 2019, https://nationalinterest.org/blog/buzz/why-loitering-munitions-are-newest-and-deadliest-threat-81241.

82   JTA, "Israeli surveillance balloon helped protect Pope in South America," The Times of Israel, September 26, 2017, https://www.timesofisrael.com/israeli-surveillance-balloon-helped-protect-pope-in-south-america/.

83   Emanuel Fabian, "Israel sends IDF team to Florida to assist with tower collapse rescue efforts," The Times of Israel, June 26, 2021, https://www.timesofisrael.com/israel-sending-idf-team-to-florida-to-assist-with-tower-collapse-rescue-efforts/.

84   "Save a Child's Heart conducts 5,555th life-saving procedure on 2-year-old Palestinian boy from Gaza," Save A Child's Heart, November 8, 2020, https://saveachildsheart.org/

news/save-a-childs-heart-conducts-its-5-555-lifesaving-procedure-on-a-2-year-old-palestinian-boy-from-gaza.

85   "SACH is First Israeli NGO to Win UN Population Award," Save A Child's Heart, June 28, 2018, https://saveachildsheart.org/news/israeli-non-profit-save-a-childs-heart-wins-un-award.

86   Nicky Blackburn, "Israel sends aid to Mexico after devastating earthquake," Israel21C.org, September 20, 2017, https://www.israel21c.org/israel-sends-aid-to-mexico-after-devastating-earthquake/.

87   Times of Israel staff, "Israeli rescue team applauded in the streets of Mexico," September 23, 2017, https://www.timesofisrael.com/israeli-rescue-team-applauded-in-the-streets-of-mexico/.

88   "Number of violent anti-Semitic attacks in 2020, by country," Statista.com, June 28, 2021, https://www.statista.com/statistics/270223/violent-anti-semitic-attacks-in-selected-countries/.

89   Ron Lee and Spectrum News NY1, "NYPD: Jewish man attacked, robbed on way to synagogue," Spectrum News NY1, July 18, 2021, https://www.ny1.com/nyc/all-boroughs/news/2021/07/18/nypd--jewish-man-attacked--robbed-on-way-to-synagogue.

90   Hayley Smith, Richard Winton, and Lila Seidman, "L.A. sushi restaurant attack is being investigated as an antisemitic hate crime," *The Los Angeles Times*, May 19, 20212, https://www.latimes.com/california/story/2021-05-19/l-a-sushi-restaurant-attack-is-being-investigated-as-an-antisemitic-hate-crime.

91   "Germany vows 'zero tolerance' for attacks on synagogues," Deutsche Welle, May 13, 2021, https://www.dw.com/en/germany-vows-zero-tolerance-for-attacks-on-synagogues/a-57521135.

92 Emily Shapiro, "New York synagogues vandalized in 'brazen' attacks, surveillance video released," ABC News, April 26, 2021, https://abcnews.go.com/US/york-synagogues-vandalized-brazen-attacks-surveillance-video-released/story?id=77316099.

93 Sophie Chong, "Toronto neighborhood home to Jewish businesses targeted with negative reviews," blogTO, June 3, 2021, https://www.blogto.com/city/2021/06/toronto-neighbourhood-jewish-negative-reviews/.

94 Walter Reich, "The Rise of Global Anti-Semitism," Wilson Center, October 22, 2014, https://www.wilsoncenter.org/event/the-rise-global-anti-semitism.

95 Wajahat Ali, "The Same Hate That Targeted Muslims Is Turning on Asian Americans Now," Beast Inside, last modified March 9, 2021, https://www.thedailybeast.com/the-same-hate-that-targeted-muslims-is-turning-on-asians-now.

96 "Hate Crime," FBI: UCR, https://ucr.fbi.gov/hate-crime.

97 Benjamin Ward, "Europe's Worrying Surge of Antisemitism," Human Rights Watch, May 17, 2021, https://www.hrw.org/news/2021/05/17/europes-worrying-surge-antisemitism.

98 "Antisemitism: A History," Counter Extremism Project, last modified November 12, 2021, https://www.counterextremism.com/anti-semitism-history/antisemitism-history/religion-and-antisemitism?gclid=Cj0KCQjw6NmHBhD2ARIsAI3hrM2q54ETuL_4ZR6j79m8nW6VRi4C8Nft87qh_qLstC_HXBN_1zUP4LkaAiFtEALw_wcB.

99 Manya Brachear Pashman, "Antisemitic Tropes Are Proliferating. Can You Spot Them?," AJC Global Voice, March 26, 2021, https://www.ajc.org/news/antisemitic-tropes-are-proliferating-can-you-spot-them.

100 Reuters Staff, "Venezuela U.N. envoy sorry for 'final solution' remarks: U.N.," Reuters, May 12, 2016, https://www.reuters.com/article/instant-article/idUSKCN0Y32RY.

101 Karen Seidman, "BDS vote stirs up hostilities on McGill campus," *Montreal Gazette,* February 25, 2016, https://montrealgazette.com/news/local-news/bds-vote-stirs-up-hostilities-on-mcgill-campus.

102 "Farrakhan: In His Own Words," ADL.org https://www.adl.org/education/resources/reports/nation-of-islam-farrakhan-in-his-own-words.

103 "A Brief History of Jews and the Civil Rights Movement of the 1960s," Religious Action Center of Reform Judaism, April 7, 2014, https://rac.org/brief-history-jews-and-civil-rights-movement-1960s.

104 "Farrakhan: In His Own Words," ADL.org https://www.adl.org/education/resources/reports/nation-of-islam-farrakhan-in-his-own-words.

105 Yitzhak Santis, "Destructive 'Agnosticism'," Haaretz, November 26, 2010, https://www.haaretz.com/1.5145058.

106 John Spritzler, "Norman Finkelstein's Criticism of BDS: Wrong, But With a Germ of Truth," NewDemocracyWorld, February 10, 2013, https://web.archive.org/web/20150612130205/http:/newdemocracyworld.org/palestine/bds.html.

107 "Anti-Semitism: State Anti-BDS Legislation," Jewish Virtual Library, last modified May 25, 2021, https://www.jewishvirtuallibrary.org/anti-bds-legislation.

108 "S.1 A Bill," Congress, January 4, 2019, https://www.congress.gov/116/bills/s1/BILLS-116s1pcs.pdf.

109 Senator Benjamin L. Cardin, "S.Res.120 - A resolution opposing efforts to delegitimize the State of Israel and the Global Boycott, Divestment, and Sanctions Movement targeting Israel," March 25, 2019, https://www.congress.gov/bill/116th-congress/senate-resolution/120.

110 Peter Baker and Maggie Haberman, "Trump Targets Anti-Semitism and Israeli Boycotts on College Campuses," *The New York Times,* last modified January 22, 2021,https://www.nytimes.com/2019/12/10/us/politics/trump-antisemitism-executive-order.html.

111 Reuters, "'Bodies all over me': Eyewitnesses recount horror in Christchurch shootings," CNA, last modified March 15, 2019, https://www.channelnewsasia.com/news/world/christchurch-shooting-eyewitnesses-recount-bodies-all-over-11347472.

112 Shannon Van Sant, "Poway Shooting Latest In Series of Attacks On Places Of Worship," NPR, April 28, 2019, https://www.npr.org/2019/04/28/718043171/poway-shooting-latest-in-series-of-attacks-on-places-of-worship.

113 Felice Gaer, "UN Finally Confronts Antisemitism As A Human Rights Problem," AJC Global Voice, October 16, 2019, https://www.ajc.org/news/un-finally-confronts-antisemitism-as-a-human-rights-problem.

114 "Simon Wiesenthal Center: Landmark UN Report on Anti-Semitism Has Potential To Be A Game Changer ," Simon Wiesenthal Center, September 23, 2019, https://www.wiesenthal.com/about/news/un-report-antisemitism.html.

115 "The Process of Othering," Montreal Holocaust Museum, last modified February 18, 2020, https://museeholocauste.ca/en/resources-training/the-process-of-othering/.

116 Iran Action Group, "OUTLAW REGIME: A CHRONICLE OF IRAN'S DESTRUCTIVE ACTIVITIES," U.S. Department of State, 2018, https://www.state.gov/wp-content/uploads/2018/12/Iran-Report.pdf.

117 Jacques Neriah and Shimon Shapira, "The Iranian Conquest of Syria," Jerusalem Center for Public Affairs, August 14, 2019, https://jcpa.org/article/the-iranian-conquest-of-syria/?mod=article_inline.

118 Iran Action Group, "OUTLAW REGIME: A CHRONICLE OF IRAN'S DESTRUCTIVE ACTIVITIES," U.S. Department of State, 2018, https://www.state.gov/wp-content/uploads/2018/12/Iran-Report.pdf.

119 "Weekend of rockets over Israel," Israel Ministry of Foreign Affairs, May 5, 2019, https://mfa.gov.il/MFA/ForeignPolicy/Terrorism/Pages/Weekend-of-rockets-over-Israel-5-May-2019.aspx.

120 Reuters Staff, "Israeli PM Netanyahu makes rare visit to Oman," Reuters, October 26, 2018, https://www.reuters.com/article/us-israel-oman/israeli-pm-netanyahu-makes-rare-visit-to-oman-idUSKCN1N01WN.

121 Loveday Morris, "Kushner presents vision of a Middle East at peace but no details how to get there," *The Washington Post,* June 25, 2019, https://www.washingtonpost.com/world/middle_east/trump-administration-touts-mideast-peace-plan-at-kushners-bahrain-workshop/2019/06/25/b13a0136-9692-11e9-9a16-dc551ea5a43b_story.html.

122 Loveday Morris and Ruth Eglash, "A Middle East mirage," *The Washington Post,* September 12, 2018, https://www.washingtonpost.com/news/world/wp/2018/09/12/feature/a-middle-east-mirage/?itid=lk_inline_manual_15.

123 Michael Crowley and David M. Halbfinger, "Trump Releases Mideast Peace Plan That Strongly Favors Israel," *The New York Times,* February 4, 2020, https://www.nytimes.com/2020/01/28/world/middleeast/peace-plan.html.